M000312564

THE DIGITAL
LIFE INSURANCE
AGENT

How to Market Life Insurance Online
and Sell Over the Phone

JEFF ROOT

The Digital Life Insurance Agent:
How to Market Life Insurance Online and Sell Over the Phone
Copyright © 2016 by Jeff Root. All rights reserved.

No part of this book may be used or reproduced in any manner whatsoever without written permission except in the case of brief quotations
embodied in critical articles or reviews. Please do not participate in or
encourage piracy of copyrighted materials in violation of the author's
rights.

Published by SellTermLife.com

ISBN: 978-0692755778

Editing by Michelle Oyler
Cover and Interior Design: James Woosley (FreeAgentPress.com)

CONTENT

PART 3: INTERNET MARKETING FOR LIFE INSURANCE SALES

PART 1

*HOW TO MARKET
LIFE INSURANCE
ONLINE AND
SELL OVER THE PHONE*

CHAPTER 1

Disruption is Happening

Technology is disrupting traditional industries in a big way all over the world. From Uber transforming the taxi industry, to Airbnb transforming the hotel industry—it's all around us. Innovative companies are using new technology to challenge the old way of doing business.

The life insurance industry is no exception.

The forces of change are already impacting our business. Most of our clients are going online to research life insurance options and get quotes. Even clients who need advanced planning are researching everything on their own.

Six-figure premium policies are being sold over the phone. Estate planning cases are being illustrated and presented online and sold over the phone.

It doesn't matter if you sell term insurance, whole life insurance, indexed universal life insurance or any other type of life insurance—the buying trends are transitioning away from the traditional face-to-face meetings. Each year, LIMRA and the Life Foundation are showing more and more consumers buying their policies online or over the phone.

There's one key thing driving this change...Time.

Most people would agree that the single most important asset anyone has is time.

Our fundamental behaviors have changed over the last decade to make "time" one of the most important factors of making a purchase.

Think about it. When your internet is slow, or you're getting poor reception on your phone, how frustrated are you? I would guess very frustrated—your time is being wasted by poor service. Besides sports, how often do you watch live TV? My hunch is not often, since now we have DVRs, Netflix and other streaming services that remove the time spent on irrelevant, boring ads.

Whether or not you realize it, technology has changed our behaviors.

Not only are we extremely protective of our time, but consumer confidence in buying online has exponentially increased over the last decade. Put those two elements together, and you'll recognize that the industry is going to keep evolving, whether or not we like it.

Fifteen years ago, about half of the American population owned a mobile phone. Today, according to Pew Research, that number is around 92%. It's safe to say that mobile phones are to stay.

You should know, too, that over 35% of our website visitors are using their mobile devices to find our life insurance websites.

This single shift in technology alone would have been enough to change how people buy their life insurance, but it's happened in tandem with many other changes.

Ten years ago I bet if someone had asked if you to enter your credit card on a website, you would have said *"There's no way!"* Today, so long as it seems trustworthy, you probably wouldn't even blink, because we've all gotten so used to online banking and other online payment processors like PayPal.

Five years ago, many people said they would never be on Facebook. Today 163 million Americans are active Facebook users, out of 323 million total Americans. That means more than half of the US population is an active Facebook user and that number is only growing. I personally know agents who are setting five or more appointments each week from Facebook ads—not leads, actual appointments. Other agents are generating leads consistently through Facebook ads as well.

Consumer confidence in researching and shopping online will continue to grow, and it's no different in life insurance.

It's critical to recognize that consumer buying behaviors are shifting because of time, accessibility and the growing confidence in the ability to buy quality goods and services online.

The evidence is in the numbers. I have personally placed over 3,000 life insurance policies over the phone since I started my business. There are life insurance agents who generate thousands of leads every month from their website(s), and they started less than three years ago. Within 12 months of diving into this new era of prospecting, agents can generate daily leads from their online presence.

Can you imagine life insurance prospects contacting you every day? How would that change your business? Your life?

One thing is clear—life insurance distribution is being disrupted. Consumers are shifting the way they're buying life insurance.

The cost of resisting this change is that you lose out on a huge pool of high-quality prospects and will never see the revenue those prospects could have injected into your business.

But if you are willing to adapt? You will get access to an unprecedented number of customers who are willing to pay for the time and convenience you can provide them. Your workflows will be smoother, you'll have more time, and you will be able to work as flexibly as you want.

The Rising Expectations of Today's Consumer

Digital technology and mobile devices have forever altered consumer expectations.

Our industry knows we need to be online to meet the rising expectations of today's consumers, but we're doing a poor job of it.

It's important to understand some major trends changing customer expectations so that we can step up to the plate and provide our customers with what they need.

Trend #1: The Rise of the 'Do it Yourself', Self-Serve Consumer

Regardless of whether you're looking for life insurance for a prospect who is a scuba diver or diabetic, a quick Google search can tell you just about anything you need to know. This means your prospects have access to nearly as much information as you do. If you don't give them what they need, they'll likely go and get it somewhere else.

While that might seem daunting, it also creates a massive opportunity for life insurance agents to get in front of the wave of consumers who are researching life insurance online.

Consumers don't have to wait to speak with an agent to get quotes on their life insurance. They don't have to track an agent down to get their questions answered. All of this is available online and a quick phone call away. You can be the person on the other end of the phone line, which means you get to be the one that sells them a policy too.

Trend #2: The Rise of the 24/7, "Always On" Expectation

Just about everyone these days has their smartphone within reach 24/7. They are connected for every waking moment to every aspect of their lives. Consumers are used to being able to find the information they need and contact whomever they want at any time of the day.

I'm not saying we actually need to be available to that degree, but your website needs to have the tools, information and resources to give your customers the impression that you're always available. When you combine this presence with useful content on your site, you are able to build trust quickly and easily with your prospects.

Agents with high-traffic life insurance websites generate leads at all hours of the day. People stay awake at night thinking about their families, so it's common to see inquiries come in at 11 p.m. or even later. Make sure your site is set up to handle those late-night shoppers.

Trend #3: The Rise of Mobile Culture

Our mobile-focused culture means customers expect websites to be "mobile friendly". They want to be able to access content from whichever device they happen to be using.

Your website should not only be mobile friendly, but mobile optimized. This means that every page should render correctly without requiring the user to "pinch" their screen to view the information.

Your quote and contact forms should be easy to find and fill out on mobile devices. Your website should load quickly on all devices, and the prospect should be able to tap on your phone number to make a call directly from their phone.

It's not only your website that needs to adapt... your communication needs to be mobile friendly too. Many prospects prefer a text to a phone call, even if it's just setting up a time to talk.

Prospects who never answered our calls or emails before are responding to texts. We have to communicate with our prospects on their preferred channel.

I get *a lot* of push-back from agents about texting their prospects. Many agents try to be respectful of their customers, and don't want to seem unprofessional or intrusive. While it's fantastic that they're so conscientious, it's important to understand that this is what many people actually want. You have have to be willing to adjust that mindset, because this really works.

Agents must start taking the mobile-focused culture more seriously. Across all of our websites, we're seeing over 35% of our traffic coming from mobile devices, and this has been steadily increasing.

The bottom line is that life insurance agents need to be giving prospects the right amount of information, accessible on their own time and be available to communicate through the channels prospects prefer.

Effective Selling

We keep hearing about life insurance ownership being at "50-year lows" and how it's a big opportunity for life insurance agents.

Our industry is trying so hard to figure out how to position life insurance as a priority for American households again, but it won't ever be back to the ownership highs in the earlier days of life insurance.

Why? Well, death isn't what it used to be.

Medicine and technology have extended our lives.

In the past, life insurance was an innovation. Families became destitute on a regular basis. People would frequently get sick and die. There were more fatal accidents. Now there are cures, medicine and technology that save many people who would have passed away—instead of dying, they survive and thrive.

Life insurance isn't as big a necessity as it was in the past, and the life insurance industry needs to realize this. More importantly, we as agents need to understand it if we want to sell as effectively as possible.

Now, this isn't all bad news for life insurance agents. Coverage is still a priority for many families and businesses—just not as big a priority as it was in the past. What we have on our side, though, is a fast-growing population, a shrinking force of life insurance agents, and new technologies to market and sell life insurance that we've never had before.

With that said, most life insurance agents waste a lot of time and energy trying to sell new clients on the *idea* of life insurance. They should be taking that same time and putting their offers in front of people who already want it.

Don't try to sell life insurance to someone who's not in the market for coverage. Sell life insurance to those who are in the buying process already, or who are great candidates for life insurance. Focus on getting in front of those people, instead of trying to force everyone to be a fit.

As previously mentioned, time is your most valuable asset. Sow your efforts in fertile ground. It might take more work to find your customer base, but it sure beats talking to people who have no intention of purchasing from you.

It's what this book is all about—providing the information and tools to find a customer base and sell to them consistently for years to come.

Importance of Marketing Online

First and foremost, agents should be marketing online because that's where potential customers are spending their time and getting their information.

According to a LIMRA report[1], 85% of consumers research life insurance online before purchasing a policy, and close to 50% of the people who bought life insurance in 2015 did so online or over the phone[2]. That's a massive opportunity that most agents are missing out on... and that trend just keeps growing.

In our business, and in the businesses of the life insurance agents we coach, the evidence of this is powerful.

In 2016, some agents have as many as one or two conversations *an hour* from online inquiries, compared to the one or two conversations *per day* that they had a few years ago.

Additionally, getting your business online is what will give you back control of your lifestyle.

The systems covered in this book teach agents how to work from anywhere, at any time, all while growing a business.

The key here is gaining flexibility in your life, while maintaining control of your business.

If you want to take your kids to school in the morning, then hit the gym and grab a coffee before starting the day, you can. If you want to take off early to catch a game with friends, you can. If you want to take an international trip in the summer with your family, you can.

---

1 - http://www.selltermlife.com/wp-content/uploads/2016/02/2015-Insurance-Barometer-2.pdf
2 - http://www.limra.com/Posts/PR/Podcasts/2013_Insurance_Barometer_Study.aspx

The internet has changed the way in which we do business. You have a golden opportunity to make the most of it.

Building a Marketing Mindset

Shortly after I got my life insurance license, I learned what is now the old-school way of prospecting. I talked to my friends and family, networked with anyone and everyone, cold-called for several hours a day, and asked my clients for referrals. Using such exhausting prospecting methods, it's no wonder why so many of the life insurance agents I started out with quit within three years.

To make my life insurance business work online I learned I had to change my mindset and let go of some of the outdated strategies that were ingrained in me during those early days.

Mindset shift #1: online marketing can take the place of *all* of that old-school prospecting.

Right now, you might feel as though you don't know enough about online marketing for this to be true in your business, but that will change quickly.

Prospecting—whether you're doing it online or offline—isn't something that comes naturally for most people. You have to learn and implement a whole new set of skills.

Educating yourself on the digital marketing strategies we'll cover in this book and implementing what you learn IS the new prospecting... and that's where the shift in your mindset needs to happen.

This educational process is *part* of your prospecting efforts, not as *taking away* from your prospecting time. Don't worry about 'being productive' here—going through the process to really learn online marketing is just as productive as cold calling a list of prospects that three other agents also just bought... in fact, it's much, much more productive.

Remember: that focused effort is much more effective than relying on natural talent.

I've trained many agents in this process over the last few years. None of them had any experience in online marketing. What they all had was a willingness to put in focused effort. They committed to learning the process and skills, which allowed them to generate hundreds of leads every month, and to eclipse competitors who had been online for much longer.

Mindset shift #2: only sell to people who want it.

You've heard it a hundred times from the old-school agents...

"Life insurance is sold, not bought."

This antiquated sales mantra assumes that you have to force the customer into buying coverage by hitting all of their emotional triggers, and pushing them to think about horrible worst-case scenarios.

This may have worked in the past, but it's not the case any longer. Consumers today want to be educated, not sold.

By offering your services online, you're completely flipping the script.

Remember: thousands of people are looking for life insurance information online *every day.*

Those people will buy from you if you can talk with them for a few minutes and answer their questions in an honest and accessible way.

If people are looking for the information, they probably want to buy. They want to get it sorted out, on their own schedule, and they'll happily do business with someone who makes the process easy for them.

• • •

In the history of selling life insurance, the most exciting, profitable time to be doing it is right now.

The advances in technology and the shifts in consumer behavior and psychology have redefined what it means to build a successful, long-term life insurance business.

You have an opportunity here that most agents throughout history could never have dreamed of. This book is going to help you capitalize on this opportunity, so you can reclaim your time, make more money, and live life on your own terms.

CHAPTER 2

Tools To Get Started

In this chapter we're going to break down the skills, tools and setup needed to make a successful transition to selling life insurance online and over the phone.

These are simple, foundational processes that can be put to use in any business. Once you've got this section sorted out, you'll be ready to start selling.

Soft Skills

These are the intangible skills that aren't usually taught in school—they're the ones acquired with life experience and practice.

Communication Skills

Selling online and over the phone is very different to doing it in person. The benefit of a face-to-face conversation with a prospect is that you get to read their expressions and body language, and adjust your message accordingly. Without those cues, you really need to hone your communications, particularly over email and on the phone.

When you're on the phone, there are a few things to keep in mind:

- Your tone carries a lot of weight. Make sure your tone is warm and friendly. Modulate your tone as well—nothing turns people off like a droning monotone on the other end of the line.

- Connect with people on a personal level. If your prospect volunteers any personal information about their family—acknowledge it, remember it and connect with it throughout the conversation. This can help replace the personal connection you get from a handshake or in-person small talk.

- If you're nervous, stand up while you're on the call. This will improve your posture and breathing, which in turn will make you sound more confident. Your level of confidence can affect *their* level of confidence, so do whatever you need to in order for them to feel like they are in safe hands.

Communication skills become even more important over email. You have even fewer cues than you do on the phone—no tone of voice, no pauses in the conversation and no personal connection.

Here's how to tackle that:

- Whenever you are communicating in writing, it's better to over-communicate. Lay out *all* the information, with explanations and asides as necessary. Make sure the prospect is crystal clear about your meaning—leave no room for misunderstandings or doubts.

- Always include resources and additional material when you can (like recorded screencasts which show the prospect the actual rates you're seeing, and links to your About Page and insurance licenses so they can get a bit more comfortable with you). Prove your expertise and back yourself up with evidence, so they feel confident about the details you're giving them.

- Inject some of your personality into your writing, and pay careful attention to the language and formatting.
    - » Make it personable and easy for your prospects to read. Use short sentences, bullet points, bold and italics, and professional but friendly language.

- Double check your grammar and spelling. Read and reread if necessary.

Organizational Skills

When you start operating online, your volume of conversations about life insurance with prospects will increase massively. Instead of a few appointments a week, you'll eventually have a few sales opportunities a day... if not every hour.

Fortunately, you don't have to spend long periods of time organizing all of these calls and keeping track of the details.

We'll discuss this more in the sales machine chapter later in this book, but here's a basic outline of how it works:

My day is organized by my CRM (customer relationship manager). It does it all for me. When I sit down at my desk in the morning, it delivers the next best lead to call and shows me all of my scheduled calls for the day. I work through the call queue, keeping it empty throughout the day, until the CRM serves up a new lead to call.

When I'm not calling, I'm marketing. Marketing is a major focus, because it's what keeps those leads coming into my CRM so that I have people to call. We'll dive into the CRM setup later in the book, along with in-depth instructions on what you can be doing to market your business.

You only need the desire to change, and the discipline to make it happen. Everything else can be taught.

Work Ethic and Commitment

This is my motto in all things, but it applies particularly well when it comes to moving your life insurance business online.

I've seen it time and time again: all you need to build a successful online agency is the desire to make it happen, and the discipline to put in the work that will get you there.

Yes, you will also need training, tools and processes. But they can be acquired—often very easily.

On the other hand, you can get all the training, tools and processes you want, but it won't build you a business unless you have the work ethic and commitment to put them to use in the first place.

The other thing people think they need more of? Time.

People tell me all the time that they just don't have time to learn online marketing. Every single time I see this as an excuse.

Like anything in life, if it's important enough, you'll make time for it.

Those agents would rather stay in their current position than endure the discomfort of rearranging their life for a while.

But if you are willing to make the time and persist through the learning curve, nothing can stop you.

Tools and Resources

Decades ago, we had no choice but to market and sell life insurance face-to-face. Because of the internet and huge evolutions in technology, we have many more options now.

The great thing about this modern era of online business is it doesn't take much money to get up and running. However, it's not free, and you should expect to have some operating costs.

Like any business, you're going to have some foundational overhead costs. Fortunately, most of these are one-off purchases you'll be able to use for the length of your career (or until the technology becomes obsolete).

There are a few tools, paid and free, which every agent needs. Once you've got them, you're in business.

- A computer, and dual monitors if possible
- VOIP phone system
- CRM (customer relationship management)
- A website for your business

Other tools you will also need:

- Quoting software, which allow you to compare rates side by side. You enter the prospect's information (such as DOB, state of residence, whether they are a smoker or non-smoker, coverage amount, and coverage length). Each piece of software will generate a quote for comparison.

- Field underwriting guides and questionnaires (these will be provided by the life insurance companies and your upline). The field underwriting guides are reference manuals for particular conditions or avocations, and the questionnaires are guides which ensure you're asking all the necessary questions when dealing with a particular condition.

- Life insurance contracts (you can get these from your upline).

- Business email. This should be set up when your website is built. It's very important for your credibility to use an email associated with your business, not an address from Gmail, Yahoo or other service providers (For example, jeff@selltermlife.com, not jeffslifeinsuranceagency@gmail.com).

Technical Set-Up

I've personally found the tools outlined above to be the most efficient options for my business. You can add or remove anything as it relates to your specific business, but I think it's helpful to have an idea of what it looks like in practice.

My personal technical set-up is the following:

- Dual monitors, with my quoting software on one screen and my CRM on the other.
    - » I open both pieces of software as soon as I get someone on the line. It really improves my

efficiency when I'm able to take notes, quote and complete applications over the phone, and then save all of that information in my CRM.

- VOIP phone.

  » VOIP allows me to make calls from my computer from anywhere with an internet connection. This lets me forward my business calls to my cell phone if I ever want to leave the office, so I can be far more mobile. I use RingCentral, but there are many comparable services out there (such as Grasshopper and Vonage).

- My preferred quoting softwares are Ninja Quoter and iPipeline, and I have both of those open in my browser tabs at all times.

  » You can purchase Ninja Quoter at NinjaQuoter. com, and your upline should give you free access to iPipeline, as it's mostly distributed to uplines.

- I keep a notebook with all the field underwriting guides and impaired risk questionnaires on my desk and ready for reference. I have them tabbed out by carrier and in alphabetical order.

  » I also have the questionnaires in alphabetical order for easier location while on the fly. In the event that someone calls in with a condition I'm not familiar with, I want to be able to confidently ask the right questions associated with their risk, and give them accurate information immediately, so my guides are always within reach.

  » You can also have them saved on your computer. You should definitely do this if you're mobile, but it's much easier to flip through a folder when you're at your desk.

- My CRM of choice has a queue-based calling system, which makes it easy for me to move from call to call, and has a robust customer profiling function.

  » Queue-based calling serves up the next best lead to call automatically based on rules you set up. I log in and start dialing whichever lead is displayed on the screen, so you never have to decide who to call next. It's really powerful when you've got a lot of leads to contact.

As I said, this is the arrangement that works for me. I'm comfortable shifting between all of these moving pieces, and as you get used to this new style of working, I'm sure you'll become comfortable with it as well.

Don't worry if it takes you a while to get the hang of it—any new system has an adjustment period. But if you stick with it for a couple of weeks, you'll be flowing through calls and applications naturally and easily.

How to Choose an Upline

An upline is an organization that sponsors an agent to sell insurance. They are the bridge between the insurance company and the insurance agent.

Uplines obtain contracts from the insurance carrier and provide them to the agent at a different compensation level to account for the necessary support services they provide to the agent.

Choosing an upline is one of the most important business decisions a life insurance agent can make, however they are not all created equally.

First, let's clarify some commonly used terms for uplines here: an "IMO" is an Independent Marketing Organization, an "MGA" is a Managing General Agent and a "GA" is a General Agent.

IMOs serve directly under the carrier and negotiate on behalf of MGAs and GAs. MGAs and GAs don't have a lot of individual negotiating power based on production, which is why MGAs and GAs partner with an IMO. By banding together, MGAs and GAs get all the services, high commission levels and bonuses the IMO offers because their cumulative production is very high for each carrier within the IMO group.

MGAs and GAs provide support and assistance to agents beyond what IMOs offer. This support typically includes sales support, underwriting support, case managers and marketing programs to help their downline agents sell more life insurance.

Many agents attempt to go directly to the insurance carrier to cut out the 'middle man', but unfortunately that's not possible with the majority of the companies out there. If you're a very high-volume producer and are willing to pay tens of thousands of dollars to an IMO, then you can cut out the MGA/GA. Typically that option isn't feasible for most agents either.

Therefore it is necessary to align yourself with an MGA or GA, but how does one choose an upline?

It's a common mistake for agents to choose their upline based solely on commission levels, but that is just one small piece of a complex puzzle. Your upline is going to have a big impact on how your business grows, so it's critical that you find an upline that offers more than just high commission levels. There are six key areas in which you'll want to assess your potential upline:

- High-risk life insurance expertise
- Sales tools
- Marketing advisory
- Support teams
- Training
- Release policy

Each of these areas can really make or break the daily progress of your business, and there are several questions in each area you should be asking any upline before you sign on with them.

1. High-Risk Life Insurance Expertise:

High-risk cases can be a very profitable part of your business. If you're able to secure coverage for high-risk clients, you will place more cases, have more consistent sales, and ultimately make more money. In order to do this, you will need the right people and processes in place. To find out if your upline has what you need, ask these questions:

Do you order your own APS?

When an upline orders their own APS, you gain a lot of flexibility in where you end up placing the policy. Many uplines won't order their own APS because it costs too much, so they have the life insurance company order the APS instead. This is important for three reasons:

- When an offer from an insurance carrier comes back declined or "approved other than applied for", your upline's underwriter can view the APS and determine if another company would take them. Your upline can't do this if they don't have the APS in house.

- If there's a better alternative than the company you initially applied with, your IMO already has the APS and medical exam in house. All that's left to do is get a signed application with the company who will take on your client's risk. A new offer can be made within two weeks, without waiting for the APS or ordering a new exam.

- The processing time is quicker. Your upline can order the APS as soon as the medical exam comes in, instead of waiting a week for the life insurance company to process and review it.

Do you provide underwriting assistance?

- Does your upline employ staff underwriters to review all the high-risk offers coming through? If not, is there someone to discuss potential high-risk cases with? If there's not someone easily accessible, you may lose out on some business. You're going to come across a lot of complex risks with which you're unfamiliar. If you have an underwriter to lean on, you'll place more business.

2. Sales Tools

Any upline can offer you contracts and commission schedules, but the best ones will give you some tools and resources to help you make more sales.

In this day and age, there is no good reason an upline shouldn't own sales technology which serves their agents. If they're not continually investing in technology, they aren't investing in you.

Make sure you ask...

How can you help me sell more life insurance?

This could be a universal drop ticket solution, exclusive products, e-signature platforms, quoting software, CRM or a full processing team to handle all of the administrative work after a sale.

All of this would help you write more life insurance business, because it's freeing up more of your time to focus on marketing.

3. Marketing Advisory

Your upline can be more than just a vendor for contracts. They should be actively helping you grow your business by sharing their marketing expertise and experience with you.

How can you help me to market my business more effectively?

I'm not talking about discounts to all of the major lead vendors. Anyone can offer discounts. I'm talking about *real* marketing advice. What do they know about marketing online and selling over the phone? Do they have any in-house lead programs? What are the marketing resources they have vetted and can refer you to?

Remember that it's your job as an agent to find your clients, not the job of your upline. That said, there are some organizations out there with deep marketing resources that can help grow your business.

It's also worth noting that as you prove your expertise and loyalty to your upline, many will include you in marketing opportunities that arise. For example, you might get involved in orphan programs (life insurance policies where the original agent is no longer active) or take part in lead partnerships that come up.

4. Support Teams

The more support your upline can provide, the better. Ideally, you'll 'outsource' all of the administrative details to their team. This includes sales support, case management and delivery requirement follow-up.

This is how agents are able to put up ridiculously high sales numbers. They're not wasting time chasing details for their cases.

Is it easy to submit and track applications through underwriting?

Your upline should make it easy to submit business, and make sure your applications are being submitted to the carrier in good order. For agents selling over the phone, I highly recommend a universal drop ticket solution. This means there's a single-page online application for all of the companies the upline offers.

Fill out one short application, and the application team takes care of getting signatures on the application (typically e-signatures) and scheduling the medical exam.

They make sure the application is completed with the right forms and in good order every single time. This eliminates the need for you to learn different applications or application processing programs whenever you write with a new company. Ask them...

Will you provide access to a portal to check on cases in underwriting?

This saves you from having to log into each carrier site and searching for your client's name when you need to check on their progress, which will save you a tremendous amount of time when things get busy.

Do you have sales support staff to help me run an illustration?

For the uninitiated, life insurance illustrations show how a permanent life insurance policy would perform in the future under a set of assumptions and guarantees. They need to be signed by your client for any permanent policies you sell them.

You're going to come across some complex cases where you'll need to illustrate a policy you're not comfortable illustrating yourself with carrier software or with Winflex (an illustration software). You'll want to lean on the expertise of the sales support staff of your upline and have them run illustrations for you.

In this situation, all you'll have to do is give the sales support staff the details of your case and they'll put together the illustration for you.

Do you provide any help on the back end for case management? If so, what does that involve?

During underwriting, the life insurance company will often ask for details or more information on what they see on the exam or medical records.

These are non-revenue producing tasks that you shouldn't be handling yourself. Utilizing the services of a case manager to fulfill underwriting requirements will save you *a lot* of valuable time.

5. Training

Your upline isn't responsible for training you on how to sell life insurance, but it's a big bonus if they do. Ask if there's any product, sales or marketing training they provide for their agent base.

In my own BGA, I teach other life insurance agents how to market online and over the phone. With my experience, I'm able to offer very specific guidance on the best methods for selling to different market segments. Your future upline may have a similar setup where someone can help train you in the areas where you need the most improvement.

6. Release Policy

Last but not least, make sure the upline has an open release policy. If you decide to leave them, the last thing you want to deal with is an upline holding your contracts hostage.

Do you have an open release policy? If not, what are the terms of release?

My rule of thumb is that if they won't release you, move on to the next upline. This is an awful business practice by upliness to hold agents hostage to their contracts.

If for some reason an upline won't release you from a life insurance company's contract, six months of no production will typically get the life insurance company to allow you move to another hierarchy.

Most life insurance companies allow dual contracting, but for those companies that don't, not getting a release can be a big inconvenience.

Non-Resident Licenses

Most agents are only licensed in the states in which they live, or one or two neighboring states.

But when you're doing business online, you're going to get people coming in from all over the country. You will need to pick up non-resident licenses to be able to serve those people, and in most states it's as simple as filling out a form.

You can get these on nipr.com and sircon.com.

Rather than applying for all of the state licenses all at once, I recommend doing it as you go. This not only spreads out the cost, but once you've submitted one application, the system will save your details, simplifying the process for subsequent applications.

I also suggest picking up perpetual licenses from the few states that offer them. As long as your home state license is valid, perpetual licenses in other states will never expire, so you never have to worry about renewing or paying additional fees.

For a list of state licenses and their corresponding fees and which states have perpetual licenses, visit selltermlife.com/book-resources.

CHAPTER 3

Field Underwriting

In this line of work, you're going to come across all walks of life. You'll talk to all kinds of people, with all kinds of diseases, medications, felonies, bankruptcies, past-times, professions... you will see it all.

To handle this kind of variety, you will need an excellent reference system. You're not expected to know everything for every type of situation, but you do need to be able to find the information quickly.

A lot of agents think they need to know it all before they start working leads and making calls, but that's a limiting belief.

No one is ever going to know it all, so don't let that get in the way of getting started. It's much easier to get the information you need as it comes up, than get stuck with no cases because you spent too much time memorizing obscure information.

The first thing you should do is print out your quick reference field underwriting guides and questionnaires. Every life insurance carrier has an agent's field underwriting guide, so collect the guides from the carriers you do the most business with, and have them ready for reference.

In addition to the field underwriting guides, you will want to have questionnaires for the most common risks printed out. Go to selltermlife.com/book-resources to download a printable .PDF copy.

The questionnaires are a key part of the process here. If someone has a health condition you're not familiar with—say, multiple sclerosis—you wouldn't immediately know which questions to ask. But with a questionnaire in front of you, you will be able to ask...

- When was your last episode?

- What type of MS do you have, Relapsing-Remitting MS? Secondary Progressive MS? Primary Progressive MS? Progressive Relapsing MS?

- What medications do you take? Injection or tablet? Dosages?

- When were you diagnosed?

Wow—it sounds like you know what you're talking about!

Be extremely organized about this: put tabs on the guides and questionnaires so that you can find each condition quickly and get started with assessing the client.

The questionnaires will make you sound like an absolute pro

to anyone you talk to. They'll feel confident that you have a deep understanding of their situation, which builds trust quickly and makes them feel comfortable pursuing coverage through you.

Non-Med Carriers

Non-med, short for non-medical, refer to the life insurance carriers that don't require a medical exam in order to provide coverage.

There are a large number of these carriers, which is highly advantageous to your business. A lot of people don't want to take a medical exam, for one reason or another, so you can make a sale simply by offering a no-exam policy.

Another reason why some individuals don't want to complete a life insurance application is time. Traditional, fully underwritten applications can take an average of four to eight weeks to get approved.

Selling no-medical exam life insurance allows you to sell a lot more policies, because many of those prospects won't fall out during the four to eight week underwriting time frame (where they have to go through the unpleasant process of getting poked with a needle, peeing in a cup, ordering their medical records and waiting around for months while someone they've never met before gets their policy together).

Try to sell as many non-med policies as you can, whenever it makes sense to do so. Print out the non-med carriers, and know their application process (many of them have their own online application) so you can close these prospects without delay.

Graded Death Benefit and Guaranteed Issue Policies

Graded death benefit and guaranteed issue policies are best for sick or unhealthy people. These are the folks who continually get declined by life insurance companies because they're too high-risk.

When you're talking to a person in this situation, you start by asking a few questions. There are usually less than 10 to go through, and they are simple yes or no health questions. As long as they answer no to those questions, they'll qualify for the graded death benefit policy.

The catch is that they won't get full coverage for the first two years. It's a graded policy, and the amount each insurance company will pay out varies for the initial period. After two years, though, they will receive full benefits.

This is a much more expensive option than regular policies, but it's often the best choice for people who can't get coverage any other way. A lot of life insurance agents don't sell these graded death benefit policies, but those who do typically make a lot of money by offering them.

Guaranteed issue policies give coverage to the policyholder, no questions asked. As long as the customer is a US citizen and is within the company's age guidelines, they can qualify for this kind of coverage.

Again, these are expensive and usually have limitations on the kind of payouts the client can expect to receive, but if the customer is in a difficult situation and needs to get something arranged quickly, a guaranteed issue policy is typically their best bet.

Quoting on the Fly

This might be one the most important skills for you to develop when you start selling over the phone. When people get on a call with you, they're going to want to hear a specific price before they hang up.

It's key to have 1) the quick-reference field underwriting guides in front of you so that you know what health classification to put your clients in, 2) the questionnaires to know what questions to ask, and 3) an instant quote program to compare quotes as necessary.

Always have these ready, and be fluent in using them. You don't want to be fumbling around while you're on the phone, clicking and typing and messing up while your prospect is on the phone. You want to be fluid so that you can get them a quote smoothly and quickly over the phone, without sacrificing accuracy.

Quick Quotes and Phone Numbers

Let's say that you have somebody who has some health conditions. You've asked them everything on the questionnaire, but you're still not sure what to rate them.

Your field underwriting guide is a bit vague, and you're not sure which health classification to put them into.

To get some help, you can email the underwriting desk at the life insurance carriers. It's called a quick quoting desk, and they'll respond back with a tentative offer.

How Does a "Quick Quote" work?

You email the underwriting desk the details of your risk. Make sure your email is as detailed as possible, so that they don't need to follow up with further questions before sending back the tentative offer.

Some carriers will respond to you on the same day, but most will reply within two business days. You can ask your upline's underwriting department for a list of the quick quote email addresses.

Some life insurance companies have underwriting desks you can call. You'll be able to speak with a real person about the risk for this client and they'll advise you on what to rate the person when they're ready to proceed.

When it comes time to complete the application with your prospect, attach the Quick Quote, as this is considered a tentative offer. As long as the information you included in your Quick Quote email matches up with everything the underwriter finds and there are no surprise risks, this Quick Quote offer will be the offer the underwriter makes.

Best Practices for Using Quick Quotes:

- Be as detailed as possible regarding health. Medications and dosages, age diagnosed, procedures with dates, etc.

- Don't use your prospect's full name. The underwriter won't reply or they'll tell you to resend your email.

- Structure the email so it's easy for the underwriter to read.

- Send one email at a time to each underwriter by copying and pasting. Do NOT mass email underwriters by putting all the email addresses in the "to" or "cc" field.

Here's an example:

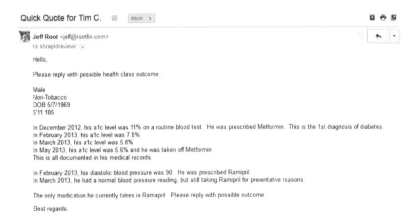

Use Your Upline

Many times, an upline will have a field underwriter on staff who you can lean on when you're in unfamiliar territory. This is particularly useful when the case is really big or complicated—getting a second opinion can ensure you have all of the details perfectly lined up.

And while the upline's underwriter can be a very useful resource, it's important that you don't get dependent on them to do your research for you.

In most cases, the research on unfamiliar conditions is something you should be doing yourself. Finding the information yourself makes it much easier for you to retain it all so that you can use it to quote future customers on the fly.

Cover Letters

When submitting a life insurance application, it's beneficial to attach a cover letter addressed to the underwriter which provides more information about a case.

If you're thinking about specializing in high-risk cases like I have, this is going to be a critical part of your success. I work high-risk cases every day, and have placed countless policies, just because I'm willing to go the extra mile and write a detailed, compelling cover letter.

Now, many agents don't know that they can write a cover letter to an underwriter, and yet those that *do* know about it are often too lazy to spend the time drafting them. Even if they do put one together, they're half-assed and ineffective.

I write cover letters for every case that has a strong possibility of being knocked back. Cover letters can get you better health classifications for your clients, which leads to better offers, which leads to more placed premium.

Scuba Diving Case Study

I had an article published on a scuba diving website which generated a few new scuba diving clients. One client in particular really needed my help. He needed a $1.5M policy to secure a loan for his business, and had an offer on the table with Prudential for $9600 in annual premium. He contacted me because of the article and wanted to see if he could get his premium lowered.

This guy was in perfect health, however he smoked pipe tobacco and dived deeper than 100 feet when he went scuba diving. The previous agent automatically went to Prudential because he could get non-smoker rates. That was a smart move, but when they did the scuba diving questionnaire, he stated he'd had two dives over 120 feet in the previous year, so Prudential rated him a Table 4.

With this information, I knew my options were limited to those companies that gave non-smoker rates for tobacco pipe use. I dove deep when questioning him about his scuba dives—where they were, how many, his certifications, how long he's been certified and so on. There was another company who would offer a Table 4 non-smoker rate as well because of the depths of his dives, but it would be more expensive than Prudential's. I knew my only shot at placing this case was convincing the underwriter to give a Standard health classification, and to let the underwriter know about the offer from Prudential.

Here's how I positioned it. I stated he only had two dives over 100 feet in the previous year, and he didn't have any definite plans to dive over 100 feet in the current year. I also explained his dives are in resort towns in crystal clear waters, he never dives in murky water, and outlined his advanced certifications. I closed the cover letter by saying if we couldn't get a Standard non-smoker offer, he wouldn't take the offer because he had another offer on the table.

Painting this picture landed me a Standard non-smoker offer for $5600 in AP. This offer was outside of their normal underwriting guidelines, but because I made his risk look a lot better than it does on paper (no scheduled future dives over 100 feet, only two dives over 100 feet in the last year, only dives in resort towns with clear water, advanced certifications), I was able to win this client. I went the extra mile and won a commission lost by another agent, just because I was willing to do a little extra work.

The Opportunity

Most of the high-risk cases running through the life insurance call centers aren't being submitted with cover letters. Some of them don't even write substandard business. This leaves a lot of high-risk people looking for better rates online for independent agents to work with.

All you have to do is qualify your prospect correctly. If your prospect has a health condition, grill them about it. Dig deep, and get *all* the information you can. If they were declined previously, don't get discouraged. Many times an agent just used the wrong company, and by delving further, you'll be able to find a company that will cover them.

Once you get ALL the details, begin your quest to find the best possible offer. Quick quote it out, talk to your upline's underwriter or ask any colleagues if they have any experience with that particular risk. Reference all the information you gathered. Once you find the right company, explain it to your prospect and if they choose to move forward, submit the case and write a detailed cover letter.

Some of my biggest cases have been high risks where my cover letter provided information that was not in the medical records, labs or application.

Life Insurance Cover Letter Tips

The purpose of a cover letter is to provide a "face" to the case, to help give the underwriter a better mental picture of the applicant's situation.

Here are some tips:

- Tell a story. Why is this coverage needed? What makes the insured a better risk than his medical records may show?

- Attach a picture if you have a prospect who is overweight, but is mostly muscle, or when their chest is bigger than their waist. Even if build isn't an issue, attaching a vibrant photo of the prospect will help the underwriter paint a picture and develop a personal association with the case. *(If the prospect is very obviously overweight, though, don't attach a picture.)*

- Divulge as much information as you can:

  » Purpose of coverage

  » How the face amount was determined

  » If coverage is for a loan, give the details on the amount and duration

  » ALL details of their health conditions painted in the most favorable light possible

  » Any daily exercise, healthy eating, daily nutritional supplements, etc.

  » Favorable lifestyle changes they've recently made

  » Any sports or physical activities

  » Any competition with another broker for the coverage

An in-depth, positive cover letter will help influence an un-derwriter's decision. A mediocre cover letter will do nothing for you, so only submit one if you plan to do it well.

Our sales duties don't stop once we've taken the application on a high-risk prospect. You now have to sell the underwriter. A cover letter is your only tool to "pitch" your client's risk to the un-derwriter, so get in the habit of writing amazing cover letters for your high-risk clients.

Informal Applications

Life insurance carriers allow you to submit informal appli-cations (also known as informal inquiries) for bigger cases. You get your client to take an exam, collect their medical records, and then submit the informal application. It doesn't go through as a complete, formal application, so you won't get an approval or de-cline, but rather a best rate quote.

It's a good idea to do informal applications for big cases only (at least $15,000 in annual premium) when there is a risk involved and you want to shop the case around. Your upline will have an in-formal application for you to complete and they'll be able to shop the case around for you.

AOTAs and Declines

In any given year, around 30% of our agency's life insurance cases will come back from the underwriter Approved Other Than Applied ("AOTA").

Approved Other Than Applied is exactly what it sounds like. It means you've submitted an application to the underwriter and they approved it as something else.

AOTAs happen to all of us. They are the result of many differ-ent things, including clients omitting facts (whether intentionally or not), or the agent not asking the right questions. The risk of getting an AOTA is just one of the reasons you must be very thorough when qualifying and quoting new prospects.

It's crucial to manage the client's expectations. If the client is prepared for the possibility of a higher rate, you're more likely to retain their business if their rates come back higher than you initially quoted. Nobody likes to feel like they've been served a bait and switch. Preparing your clients for the possibility will help avoid that.

If an application comes back AOTA, you need to handle it gently. This is very sensitive, and can be uncomfortable for the client. And remember—you don't get paid until the policy is paid. Getting an AOTA is a major cause of clients walking away and doing business with someone else, or not securing coverage at all, so this is critical for you to understand.

Now, before we get to the actual conversation to have with a client who received an AOTA, there are three ways you can move the policy forward in a more satisfactory way:

1. See if they can get a better health classification or rate with another carrier.

2. Reduce the coverage amount.

3. Reduce the term of the coverage.

With this in mind, here's how to approach the client on the phone:

1. State that you have good news. They've been approved, though there are some variations from the original quote. *Before going into the details, restate their motivation for getting this coverage from your original conversation.*

2. Explain the reason for the AOTA—make sure you have the specifics from the carrier if available.

3. Reaffirm why they need this coverage, and why it's valuable to their beneficiaries.

4. Outline the three options above and ask them to make a decision—right now—about how to proceed, so you can inform the carrier or start moving on other options. Have them act right away. *If they need to confirm with a spouse, ask them for their anticipated answer so you can let the carrier know and then have them call back to confirm. It's important to make them call you back, not vice-versa, so they are mentally committed to the process.*

5. Stress the fact you can get coverage in force today to protect their family, and pursue other options at the same time.

You can say something like: "I recommend taking this offer to protect your family today, and I'm willing to assist you in reapplying when you get your cholesterol and blood pressure under control again."

In another scenario, you could say: "You mentioned you needed at least $1,000,000 of coverage. Why don't we drop the term from 20 years down to 10 years to get the rate lower, and then re-apply next year?"

On this call, make sure that you exude confidence. After all—they were approved! Also make sure you drive the call and don't let your client take over. It's important to get a decision here and keep the momentum up, so you don't lose their business. If there's a big variation in the AOTA, say, at least four health classes below what you initially quoted, here's another strategy you can use:

STEP 1/DAY 1

"Mr. Client, I just wanted to let you know that ABC company approved your policy but they increased the rates and I am not satisfied that we have a good offer here. I wanted to let you know that today I am preparing to send your case out to several other carriers to see if we can improve your offer. Give me three to four days and I will know more." **DO NOT GIVE PRICE, NO MATTER WHAT.**

STEP 2/DAY 2 OR 3

"Mr. Client, I have offers back from Company A, Company B and Company C and all are approving the same health class. I haven't run pricing with any because I am still waiting on Company D and Company E and am holding out hope they will approve a better rate. I should have their responses within a day or two and will be in touch." **DO NOT GIVE PRICE, NO MATTER WHAT.**

STEP 3/DAY 4 OR 5

*"Mr. Client, OK—I have all the offers back from the other carriers, and I am now satisfied we are working with a good offer. At this point, **we have to make it work because it is absolutely the best you are going to get.** After speaking to several underwriters, based on your A1C of 6.7, we are looking at what is called a Table 2 rating. Of 16 categories a person can qualify for, this means you are number six."*

Then provide their options, and have them decide on coverage or term period in order of importance.

Declines:

If a life insurance company flat out declines your client, don't give up.

Your first course of action would be to see if a "reconsideration request" is warranted.

In this situation, you want to get as much information as you can about the decline from the insurance company.

If you find some of the decline reasons are wrong or are based on misinformation, try pushing back on the insurance company (particularly if you have updated information) and ask them to reconsider. Often times a letter from a physician clarifying one of the reasons for the decline can turn a decline into an approval.

If the decline was due to the medical exam results and your client is surprised by them, tell the life insurance company that this doesn't measure up with your client's last physical. Ask if they would reconsider if the client took another exam, as many times the life insurance company will say yes to this (provided the second exam is at the expense of your client).

If a reconsideration request isn't an option, then check to see if other carriers would approve this risk. Have your upline look at the APS and determine if there are other alternatives.

If there are no other alternatives, offer your client graded death benefit coverage, guaranteed issue coverage or accidental death and dismemberment (AD&D) coverage.

And if there is no viable option with those products, set a follow-up based on your client's situation. Let them know what needs to happen in order for them to secure coverage and follow up based on those conditions.

For example, if they have elevated A1C levels and they'll need two follow-up visits to the doctor showing controlled A1C levels over six months, then follow up in six months to check in.

The worst thing you can do is just mark the client as a dead lead and never follow up again. Coach them on what they need to do to secure coverage and keep following up.

CHAPTER 4

Selling Over the Phone

As your business moves away from the traditional face-to-face method, the phone is going to become one of your main sales tools. In this chapter, we're going to cover the key strategies you'll need when it comes to actually closing sales over the phone.

Your leads will have completed a form online, so you know they're interested and want to buy coverage. The advice in this chapter will help you write more business without ever seeing the person in the flesh.

As we discussed earlier, there are a couple of simple things you can do to make sure your calls are as effective as possible:

Firstly, make sure your tone is warm, friendly and modulated. Nothing turns people off like a droning monotone on the other end of the line.

Secondly, if you're nervous, stand up while you're on the call. This improves your posture and breathing, which in turn makes you sound more confident. Your level of confidence affects *their* level of confidence, so do whatever you need to do in order for them to feel like they are in safe hands.

This is your baseline, but there are seven key methods that ensure you have the best possible success on all of your sales calls.

Seven Methods of Successful Life Insurance Telesales Agents

Note: Todd Ewing contributed significantly to this section. His insights into positioning are invaluable, and I'm really happy to have been able to include his expertise in this book.

Method 1: Develop Rapport and the Role of Advisor

First things first—let's talk about rapport. This is a critical sales skill, but people mistake building rapport for just being nice to clients. Building rapport is not about being nice, or being their friend. It's about being an expert. It's about being their trusted advisor.

People buy from people they trust. Buying life insurance is a big decision, so prospects will always choose somebody they feel is trustworthy and an expert.

When making calls, an agent must immediately establish credibility, authority and expertise.

It's paramount that the customer sees you as successful and professional, and you must convey that from your first spoken words. That's why the opening segment of your presentation is critical. The sale can be won or lost in the first two minutes, and there's no second chance at a first impression.

To set a strong frame for every call, you should use a strong opening line that is clear, articulate and authoritative. Use your name, and speak in a paced, warm tone. Present your title confidently, mentioning that you are licensed in your prospect's state. Finally, capitalize upon the lead source—mention the partnership or platform that the lead came through.

Once you've established who you are and why you're calling, it's time to move on to establishing rapport:

- Don't engage in excessive small talk. No one cares about the weather when they are shopping for life insurance.

- Affirm their need for life insurance with confidence. Use the data they shared in the online form to direct the conversation.

- Start "tonal modeling" based upon their speech patterns. If they speak quickly, speed up a little. If they speak slowly, slow down a bit. Subtly mirror their language and tone.

- Ask if they've used your services before to save on their life insurance. This positions you as an authority, as well as probing whether they're new to life insurance.

- Ask for the reason why they're buying a new policy. *("What's come up in your life that made you realize you need to secure new coverage?")*

- Ask the name of their beneficiary, and then refer to that person frequently.

- Pave the way to a double sale. *("Are we looking at life insurance rates just for you? Or someone else as well?")*

Once you've built rapport and know their motivations, they'll be ready for you to get into the details.

Ask them to get a pen, so they can write down all the details: *"I'm going to give you detailed information, so let me know when you're ready"*. This engages them and avoids the "could you send me this in writing?" objection.

Once they're ready, it's time to perform a needs analysis. Start by asking your prospect, *"How did you come up with [their stated amount] of coverage?"*

If they don't know how much coverage they need or don't know why they need the amount of coverage they're asking for, complete a further needs analysis.

You will notice here that we are not suggesting completing a full-blown needs analysis every time. One of the main reasons is time. Our prospects are busy people, and it is difficult to ask someone to spend even more time with you over the phone. We don't have the advantage of sitting down in their living room as if we were their financial planner.

Now, many prospects will try to rush you, but you need to take control of the call. Remember—you're an authority and an expert. You're on par with their doctor and attorney, so don't let them hurry you.

The next element of the presentation is a smooth transition to your value proposition, which is covered in Method 2.

Method 2: Deliver Your Value Proposition

It's essential that you differentiate yourself from the other life insurance agents out there. Why should this customer buy from you? What is the benefit to them by choosing you?

The customer needs to feel confident that your experience and expertise will generate their best outcome—and you must believe in order to be believed. If you don't truly believe you're going to do a great job for your customer, they won't either. Make sure you're confident in your ability to deliver results for them.

If you're selling a more expensive product, then make sure you know the value and can communicate it to your customer. What are the intrinsic qualities associated with it which makes it more expensive? Alternately, if you sell low-cost products, let them know that they're not going to get a better rate anywhere else.

Once you've done the needs analysis, you need to spend some time building up their trust in your company, rather than just launching into the health questions:

1. Use transitional lines to start talking about your company:

- "Since you're new to shopping for insurance, let me tell you a little about our company."

- "Since you're looking to save money on a new policy, let me tell you how we make it easy to get your best prices."

- "You may have read about us online. Here's how we can help you save even more."

2. Share three points that make your company seem strong and trustworthy:

You want to know your elevator pitch like the back of your hand, and be able to deliver it powerfully. This is often what gets a customer's attention and locks them in with you.

- "We're one of the nation's largest insurance brokerages."

- "We've been in business since..."

- "We've helped hundreds of thousands find their 'best buys.'"

- "We offer unique, innovative and best of class products."

- "We make insurance simple, easy and affordable."

3. Segue into your company's unique value proposition:

This is where you let the customer know what differentiates you and your service from your competition. Here are a couple of segue phrases:

- "Of the 1400 insurance companies in the industry, we work with the top providers to offer the best combination of quality, service and price."

- "We only represent the top [one percent of the marketplace/your niche here] to offer high-quality protection at the lowest prices."

4. Create urgency:

Urgency is a powerful motivator. Try to impress upon the prospect the importance of buying soon, particularly if they're unwell, have small children or are the sole income provider for their household.

- They *need* to have protection—it's their responsibility to their family.

- Life insurance rates are at all-time lows but could go up at any time. If their birthday is around the corner, the price may be going up, so they must take advantage of "save age" and "backdating" tools.

5. Transition into carrier inventory:

Remember your prospects don't know who you are to begin with. They don't know your company, so naming the brand-name companies you work with will help put them at ease:

> *"All the companies we represent are rated A and above and they provide the most comprehensive coverage. These are companies you know and trust like MetLife, Prudential, Banner Life Insurance, and North American."*

Soften the question session with a transition:

"Every company looks at your background differently, so we need to ask some questions to match you with the right company who will offer you the best value."

Method 3: Master the Qualification and Underwriting Section

Good underwriting requires you to ask very detailed questions—far beyond the bare minimum many agents stick to.

Height, weight and smoking will get you started, but what about depression? What about their driving record? What about pilot's licenses, or scuba certification, or other ancillaries? The more questions you ask, the more accurately you'll be able to select an appropriate product for them, which in turn makes it more likely they'll be approved as applied for.

It's important here that you don't 'lead the witness'. Avoid asking questions like *"You don't have any health problems, right? Nothing like diabetes, or cancer, or heart conditions?"*

Those questions create an environment where the client doesn't want to disclose those details, and you won't get the data you need to accurately place their application. Just ask the questions very clearly and don't show any reaction to what you're told.

Just gather the data and make sure you ask all the questions. Show them respect, but don't rush through the questions.

In order to find the right product for each client, it's absolutely essential to master carrier-specific nuances. These are the differences between the carriers that will determine which company is the best fit. Having this knowledge on hand enables you to speak with conviction and to demonstrate your expertise.

Some real-world facts for you to keep in mind:

- According to LIMRA data from 2013, the top three reasons for AOTAs (Approved Other Than Applied) in the industry are height and weight, hypertension and elevated cholesterol/HDL ratio. The majority of AOTAs are not caused by 'surprises' from the lab results.

- The industry average for coverage being returned AOTA is 25%-30%.

- Only 50% to 60% of AOTA's go paid. In contrast, 85%-95% of "approved as applied" go in-force.

- Over 60% of apps submitted are "Preferred Plus", but only 30% of clients ultimately get that rate!

- An improper risk assessment or choosing the "wrong" carrier will probably result in a lost sale. If sold, you will potentially "penalize" the PI thousands of dollars during the policy, for *your* error.

Most customers don't know the complexities of underwriting and how insurance pricing works. *It's your fiduciary responsibility to inform and educate them.*

On every call, you should...

- Ask all of the required questions, and explain the reason you're asking:
    - » *"Every company looks at your background differently, so I need to ask you some questions to match you with the right company who will offer you the best value and the best price for your situation."*

- Share all the carrier inventory options, and inform the client how prices are evaluated.

- Demonstrate your expertise, by matching the client with the right product and price for their specific needs.

If you can provide all those elements, you will close more sales, build better rapport, increase your credibility, and distinguish yourself from your competition. You'll improve your customer experience, reduce AOTAs, and increase your placement ratio... not to mention that you'll generate more premium, and make more money. If you can master Method 3, you'll hear "yes" more often when you present the rates to close the sale.

Method 4: Present the Rates

This part is most probably why you got into sales. There's nothing more satisfying than closing a sale you've worked hard for.

Mastering Methods 1, 2 and 3 allows you to run the earlier part of the call without needing to focus too hard on it. You can save up your energy to present the right company and rate for their *unique* needs in a way that really engages them at this critical point.

Before you present the rates, make sure you frame the offer carefully, getting as much buy-in from the client as possible:

> *"I've got everything I need based on everything you told me. So while we're searching for the best rates I'm curious, Mr. Johnson, what's most important to you? Are you looking for the highest quality protection? Do you want the top rated company? Do you want the rock bottom, lowest price? Do you want the fastest processing, the quickest way to get a policy? Or some combination of all of them? What's most important to you?"*

These questions allow you to position the offer according to their priorities, which makes it very easy for them to say yes.

Once you're ready to present the rates, use this framework to direct the conversation:

1. "Ok, if you have your pen handy, here are the best rates..."

2. Give the name of the carrier and background *before* giving the price. Present the offers with conviction, highlighting why each one is a great fit for the client.

3. Provide both monthly and annual rates.

4. Allow time for the client to respond. If they are hesitating, you can offer them an "A/B choice"— whittle down the choice to the most important element of each. Or you can tell them which one *you* would choose if you were in their position. When they engage, you can use an assumptive close to get them over the line.

5. Close with "In order to get this policy for (Beneficiary), it's a simple process..." and then go on to make the necessary arrangements.

This process will become smoother over time, as you get more used to selling over the phone and anticipating how people will respond. If you are getting a pattern of objections after the rate presentation, go back to Methods 1 and 2 to practice laying the groundwork more effectively.

Method 5: Address Objections

Regardless of how much your prospects need coverage, you're going to get objections from time to time. People frequently put off difficult or expensive decisions, so you need to be prepared to help them get across the line. There are a few steps you can take to get a prospect past their objections, without making them feel like you're pushing them too hard.

Step 1: Isolate the Objection

Make sure the objection you're hearing is the *real* reason they're not moving forward right now, and not just a smoke screen.

Here's how you can isolate an objection:

> **Client:** *"I need to speak with my spouse about this."*
>
> **Agent Isolation:** *"I completely understand, I would do the same with my spouse. Let me ask you, if you did speak with your spouse and they were okay with everything we discussed, is there any other reason we wouldn't apply for this coverage?"*

Any answer other than "yes" means this wasn't the real objection.

Once you know what the real issue is, you can address that objection. Usually they need some more information or have some kind of trust issue with the situation.

Step 2: Address the Objection

There are five common objections that come up on calls again and again. Knowing how to handle them smoothly will help you close a lot more business.

1. It's Too Expensive.

Let them know you're looking at the company that will view their application most favorably, and that they're not going to find a better rate for the amount of coverage they want.

You can ask them: *"What's more important to you—the face amount of the policy, or the length of the term?"* By altering either one of those, you can lower the rate.

You also have to gauge their interest: if this excuse is a smoke-screen and they don't actually want to buy, nothing you offer them is going to make them bite. However, if they *are* interested and it's really too expensive for them, you can work together to find some middle ground that gives them good coverage in a price range they can afford.

To really get a good picture of their financial situation, you can ask:

- How much their income is.

- How much time is left on their mortgage.

- How much their mortgage was for or how much their monthly payments are.

You can quickly tell from these questions if the prospect is going to have a pricing issue, which will allow you to tailor how you present rates to them. If you know they are living paycheck to paycheck, and the monthly coverage is $80, you can preface it by saying...

> *"This is a customized amount, and gives you the appropriate amount of coverage. The number I'm about to share with you is about 1.2% of your total income, but what you're trading for that 1.2% is the peace of mind that comes from knowing your mortgage will be paid off, and your kids won't have to move out of the family home after losing you. If you were to pass away tomorrow, you would know your beneficiary is going to be taken care of. They'll be able to pay the bills and feel safe and secure, so it's one less thing they would have to worry about while they're coping with your loss."*

Then you can give them the price, knowing they can afford it, and having framed it as a tiny percentage of their income that will yield a huge benefit to them. You do have to do some work during the call to get a clear picture of their finances, but this is a highly effective way to get people to see past the dollar amount.

If they still object to the price after that, the issue is probably not actually about the price. At that point, you have to read between the lines. One option is to ask them what is the amount of premium they would be comfortable paying. When they give you a number, say $70 for this example, you can ask them:

"If I can get you this coverage at $70 per month, would you apply today?"

If they say yes, you know the objection is about price, and you can find the middle ground for them.

If they say no, then you know there's something else you need to address.

2. I Need To Think About It

A prospect who makes this objection is really telling you they don't have enough information to feel comfortable making a decision. To deal with this particular objection, you can ask them point-blank:

"What is the particular part of this you need to think about?"

If you're getting that objection frequently, you may need to adjust the script you use earlier in the call to give more information to your prospects up front. Life insurance is not a "think about it" decision.

If you've addressed all the details a prospect could possibly need to buy coverage and they still want to think about it, it's time to ask them what the real problem is.

- What are they uncomfortable with?
- What isn't clear to them in this process?
- What is the deep concern they're not telling you about?

You can frame this conversation around the inherent risk we all face each day:

> *"Tomorrow is promised to no one. We don't know when we'll take our last breath and leave our family with the financial burdens we currently have.*
>
> *Think about the reason you're buying coverage and what would happen if you weren't around tomorrow. It's fresh on your mind so lets take care of this. You can cancel at any time if you feel there's a better product for you out there."*

Put it back on them, and show them the ramifications of taking too long to think about it. That perspective can remove a lot of resistance.

At the beginning of your conversation, it's key that you ask them why they are looking for coverage. That way, if they say they need to think about it, you can link it back to their primary motivation:

> *"It's great you want to think about this and make sure you make the right decision for your situation. As you know, we've found the company who will give you the best rates, and as it stands, the approval process usually takes around four to eight weeks. Why don't we submit the application, so you have at least four weeks to think about whether you do want to go ahead with the coverage.*
>
> *It doesn't cost you anything to put in the application, and it gives you time to think about it while the insurance company also thinks about it. That way, if you do decide you want to go ahead, you're not exposed for two more months before the policy comes through."*

3. I Need to Speak to My Spouse.

This is very similar to "I want to think about it". It usually means they're not ready to make a commitment—either they don't have enough information or they don't intend to buy.

Sometimes, they really will need to confirm with their spouse. If that's the case, tailor your according to whether you're speaking to a man or a woman.

If you're speaking to a man, you can ask:

> *"Do you really think your wife is going to be opposed to you putting a life insurance policy in place to protect the family in case you pass away? I don't think she will, and I've never had a wife call me up and say she was mad about her husband trying to do the right thing by the family. Why don't we put the application in, get the process started, and if some for some reason she objects, we can always withdraw the application. How does that sound?"*

If you're talking to a woman, you can say:

> *"Look, I don't want this to drag on and take days and days of your time. My wife and I only see each other about three hours a night, and talking about life insurance is not a priority when we're trying to get the kids to bed, get them ready for school the next day, and actually have some time together.*
>
> *What I would rather do for you is to get the application submitted so you have plenty of time to talk to your husband about it, and if anything changes in the next few weeks, you can just call me. If you don't need it anymore, I can pull the application for you—it's no extra effort on my part.*

What I don't want to see is you putting it off until you've forgotten about it, and then having to go through this whole long process again when you really need the coverage."

4. I'm Just Shopping Around for Quotes At the Moment

You'll often get this one right at the beginning of a call. The prospect thinks they're doing you a favor by letting you know they're not planning to buy today.

If it happens at the beginning of the call, you can say:

"No problem, I understand. I'm a consumer just like you. I represent all the best life insurance companies, so I'll be able to walk you through who is going to look at your application most favorably when you're ready to go ahead."

Once they've gone through the call with you, though, they should have a clear picture of how valuable the coverage will be, how competitive your rates are, and what good service they will receive from you throughout the whole process.

If it happens at the end of a call, though, then your script might need work. At that point, you have to convince them that these are the best rates and they're not going to get anything better.

You can phrase it like this:

"Listen, I do this all day, shopping for all kinds of life insurance policies. You can think of me as your personal shopper. I'm an unbiased source, because I work <u>with</u> insurance companies, not for them. I'm showing you the prices from the top insurance companies."

When you present the rates, share your screen with your prospect, so that you see the results at the same time they do.

This allows them to see the exact amount of coverage and the big brand-name on the screen. It builds trust quickly, and shows them they are getting great rates with you. There's no way for them to argue that you're not giving them the best results they can expect to find. Join.Me is a great tool for this.

5. I'm Not Interested

You can just steamroll this objection. They came to your site and filled out a form, so you know it's a smoke screen. No one is filling out those forms just for fun.

Here's what you say:

> "It's life insurance! No one wants it! It's the only product you ever buy and hope to never use. You have to have it though—imagine if your family had no financial security in place, because you were no longer in place."

Then you just push straight through:

> "The purpose of my call is to connect you with the insurance companies who can provide you with the right coverage for your family, and to take the frustration out of the process of applying."

Don't get hung up on "not interested." Just keep talking—the next few things you say will change their mind, so don't let them interrupt.

This is not as common as the other objections, because most prospects *are* interested if they've stayed on the phone with you. So you know that if this one comes up, you can call them out.

It can be uncomfortable the first few times, but steamroll this one. Stick to a script that works and address the real fears and motivations of the prospect.

Remember: objections are simply opportunities to hone your skills and master these seven methods.

Method 6: Secure the Sale

Once the customer agrees to starting an application, it's essential you affirm their buying decision. Sending an app out means nothing if the client doesn't end up actually buying a policy, so it's key to impress on them what a smart decision they're making.

By obtaining all the required information and properly explaining the ensuing process, you will also significantly increase your placement ratios.

The best agents are able to make the client's next steps sound simple and easy, while confirming their commitment to completing the whole process.

Everything from this point needs to be positive. Framing each step in the process from this point as "simple", "easy," hassle-free," or "fast" will help keep the client moving forward.

After getting a "yes" to the application, continue your conversation by...

1. Voicing a positive affirmation of their smart buying decision.

2. Asking all the required questions to send a "complete" application.

3. Demonstrating your mastery of the application system (to minimize talk time).

4. Accurately describing the "approval process".

5. Asking for payment with confidence and convey protection benefits.

6. If an E-Signature is required, completing the process while on the call.

7. If replacing an existing policy, reminding them not to cancel until their new coverage is approved.

8. Creating urgency to complete any further requirements in a timely way.

There's nothing better than the customer confirming they understand and are committed to getting their policy. If you encounter any objections at this stage, you must address them before sending the application: getting a paid policy is your priority!

Getting that client confirmation is critical to mastering Method 7.

Method 7: "Wrap-up" and "Tie-down"

To make sure the policy stays on the books, you need to use "tie-downs" to direct the customer's next steps.

Your approach here, while courteous, needs to be both instructive and direct. Tell them what happens next, and what they need to do to push their coverage through.

For each step, make sure you're *giving* information and *getting* confirmation:

1. Spin all the positives and make them aware that you're doing most of the work.

2. Provide tips on taking the exam. Tell them to fast for 8 hours prior to the exam and the easiest way to do that is schedule the exam for the first thing in the morning. Drink plenty of water and know all your doctors and medications. Be on their side as if you want them to get the best rate possible.

3. Define timelines and create urgency with birthday, need, save age, savings, etc.

4. Provide a final recap of their new coverage. Explain everything the beneficiary will get, in order to make the coverage real to them.

5. Let them know they can call anytime with questions, and that you're happy to speak with their beneficiary as well.

6. Tell them about your "assistant" and case management team, particularly if someone other than yourself will be in touch to book the exam or get additional details. This manages their expectations and makes your company sound big and stable.

7. Ask for referrals: *"Who else in your family and friends could I help?"*

8. Thank them for their business.

Find a great last line to wrap everything up professionally and positively. At this point, you have an opportunity to connect on a more personal level. Your customer should feel like they have a new agent they can trust. They're done shopping and should feel really good about their coverage.

Master Phone Sales

Trust Is Key

Trust is the only thing that really matters in sales—if you can't get the person to trust you, you won't get an opportunity to deliver the result they are looking for. To that end, you need to get to know the client over the phone before you try to give them any quotes. The best way to do it is to start with a simple question:

"Why do you want this coverage?"

Find out what has motivated them to buy life insurance at this time. As you know, there are all kinds of reasons people decide to get coverage, but asking them about it does a couple of things:

- It puts them in a conversational frame of mind.

- It allows you to build rapport up front, increasing the likelihood they will trust you.

- You get to rely on the information they give you as you progress through the sales process.

This is such an important part of the conversation that I won't even move forward with looking at quotes until the customer has answered this question.

If they can't tell me the purpose of the coverage, one of two things is happening: they are unwilling to trust me, or they're using me to get information they don't want to find themselves.

Neither of those situations will ever lead to a sale, so this initial question is a critical filter. If they do answer the question, though, you immediately start building the trust and rapport that's needed in order to make a sale. You can refer to their motivation throughout the call, reminding them of the purpose of the coverage if they have any objections or hesitations.

Some other ways to build trust include...

- If they're in front of their computer, do a screenshare with them. As mentioned in Method 5, show them the actual rates you are seeing and comparing, so they feel reassured that you're being completely transparent.

- If they're not in front of their computer, you can send them screen recordings of the quote comparisons with software like Jing or SnagIt. Just explain the comparisons you're making, so they can see exactly what you're doing for them.

- At the least, you should send them some screenshots of the rates you've found for them. Any external evidence of your efforts should be shared with the customer.

Transparency is critical for life insurance agents. People are wary of being ripped off or ending up with the wrong kind of coverage. Even a hint of 'funny business' and their trust in you will evaporate instantly.

Do everything you can to reassure them you're in their corner and working your hardest to get the policy that's best for them.

Once you've built some trust, you can move forward into exploring what kind of coverage they will qualify for. The questions can get into sensitive territory—you're going to be asking them about their family history, their height and weight, their medications, their criminal and financial history—all on the first phone call.

Now, if people trust you, they'll give you all the information you ask for. But if they don't, they'll either avoid giving you anything, or they'll give you incomplete information. You need *all* the details to be able to give them accurate quotes... so make sure you've done the work to earn their trust first.

Once you've got all the details, it comes down to what they can afford. Again, you need the customer to trust you in order for them to feel comfortable discussing this with you.

Use Scripts and Outlines

In the beginning, when you're starting out with phone sales, you should say the same thing every time. Use a script, so you don't stumble over your words, you don't lose your place in the process, and you don't start going off on tangents.

Now, you don't want to sound like a scripted robot. You don't need to memorize it, or read from it word for word, but you should have it printed out in front of you so you can follow along smoothly.

When you feel comfortable with the process—and that might be in a few days, a few weeks or a few months, depending on your personality and experience—you will be able to do your calls without needing the script so much.

That's when you should switch over to following a 'call outline'. Call outlines will help you to stay on topic, cover everything necessary to build trust and ensure your presentation is effective—without making you sound robotic.

It's key for you to stay on topic, but also that you connect warmly with people and allow the conversation to flow naturally. As long as you use the script or an outline, you'll be able to make this happen.

Now, a lot of people take issue with using scripts. They think it makes them sound robotic or unprofessional, but to be successful you have to be prepared. You have to know what to say, how to say it and when to say it. If you use this roadmap on every sales presentation, it will become second nature to you and it won't sound like a script.

Here's the basic outline of an effective sales script:

- Introduction
- Purpose
- Who We Are
- Establish Need
- Prescreen (Qualifying questions)
- Quote Presentation

This process breaks the ice, builds rapport and trust, qualifies the lead, and tells them who you are and why you're the right choice for them.

We use scripts for consultative selling, and for assumptive selling.

Consultative Selling

In our business, we've closed thousands of sales using this script and language.

I'm going to break down the script to show you the reason we say what we say. Let's start with the introduction and purpose of the call.

> *"Hi Bill, this is Agent Schrader calling from DEA Insurance following up on your request for life insurance. Did I catch you at a bad time?"*

You may notice we don't ask for the prospect by their last name. We find it's more personal and less "salesy" when we ask for the prospect by their first name.

By asking the question "Did I catch you at a bad time?", you're showing your prospect that you value their time. And by asking the question in this particular form, the most natural answer will be "no" which is what you need to proceed.

Now you want to immediately ask for the "double" and say:

> *"Great. We'll just need a few minutes with you to provide an accurate rate and answer any questions you may have. By the way, are you looking for life insurance for yourself or is this for your spouse as well?"*

They'll respond as appropriate, but what's important is that by asking for the "double", you show them you're trying to take care of their needs. This will also increase your sales, and needs to be asked to every life insurance prospect.

Then go into "who we are."

> *"Sounds good. Just to give you some background on our agency:*
>
> *We're a life insurance comparison service and will shop over 60 of the nation's top rated life insurance*

companies, including Prudential, MetLife and ING just to name a few.

The most important thing to understand is we work on behalf of YOU and not any life insurance company to find the best rates available on the market."

The purpose of this section is to establish trust and credibility around the companies that we represent, but also with you as their agent.

If you don't have their trust you don't have a sale.

"First off, are there any questions you have for me?"

Give them the opportunity to state any questions or concerns. Questions left unanswered can turn into objections later. By asking this question you're also making it more of a conversation instead of a "presentation".

Next we need to establish the need.

"So, what's come up that's prompted you to want to buy life insurance?"

This is the single most important question to ask your prospect. You're getting them to state the reason they're purchasing the policy out loud. You'll want to repeat and affirm the reason throughout your presentation to remind them why they need life insurance.

Once they answer this question, there's a real connection between you and the prospect, and the rest of the conversation flows much better since you understand their situation.

The reason we use the terminology of "what's prompted you to want to buy life insurance" is because it means they're essentially agreeing—yes, they do want to buy life insurance.

Follow up this question by asking:

"Do you currently have life insurance in force?"

If they answer yes:

> *"Are you looking to replace or add to an existing policy?"*

We ask this question for several reasons. There's an opportunity to upsell if they're looking to add to their existing policy by potentially replacing their current coverage. Ask how much coverage they have, the length of the term, year it was purchased, the carrier and the premium. It may make more sense to replace their old policy with a new one totaling the amount they desire, which will result in a higher commission.

If they answer no:

> *"Oh, okay! I'm glad I can help you (insert reason for insurance) TODAY."*

The power behind this response is your inflection. You want to act surprised they don't already have coverage, and reaffirm the reason for their purchase: "Oh! Okay, I'm glad I can help you (protect your family) today." The inflection implies that insurance should already have been in force and that it's imperative it's purchased today.

After establishing the need, we transition to the pre-screening process. You'll say:

> *"The most important thing to understand when shopping for life insurance is that each life insurance company will look at you differently. The key to securing the best life insurance rates is finding the company who will look most favorably at YOUR individual health and lifestyle. Does that make sense?"*

This is the single most important point of the process You need them to acknowledge this, which is why you ask if it makes sense.

You need to make sure they know that qualifying for the rates they see on TV or some insurance websites isn't always possible. There's a lot of information and research involved, so you need to convince them you are an expert and know the industry inside and out. That way, when you present the rate they will understand it is specifically tailored to their health and lifestyle.

> *"So, I'm going to ask you some basic questions to make sure we get you an accurate quote. Please be as open and honest with me as possible so I can find the lowest rates available."*

It's important to have them be completely honest. If they withhold or misrepresent information, it can result in an inaccurate quote, which in turn can lose the sale down the road. Gather as much health data as possible.

Now you've figured out if they even qualify for life insurance, you move into the needs analysis portion of the script by asking:

"How much life insurance are you looking for?"

Follow up immediately with:

"How did you come up with that amount?"

If they don't know how much coverage they need or don't know why they need the amount of coverage they're asking for, complete a full needs analysis.

If they are confident in the amount they are seeking, then you can move forward.

Next you need to gather how long of a term they are looking for.

"How long a term did you have in mind?"

Some people may know exactly what length of term they need. Some may be open to suggestions, and the reason for the insurance usually will determine the length of the term. For example, if they're purchasing their coverage to protect their family, they usually purchase a term to cover their kids until they are financially independent, or until the prospect has reached retirement age. However, the term they actually purchase is usually based on their budget.

At this point move on to shopping the rate and go for the close:

> *"As a reminder, I'm shopping over 60 life insurance companies and I'm finding the best rate for a 20-year, $500,000 policy is with Prudential for $62 per month. MetLife is $67 per month, and the other carriers are higher... do you have a preference?" (PAUSE)*

The value of this statement is it shows you are impartial and, as promised, shopped the market to find your prospect the very best rate possible.

You're also assuming the sale. You need to ask "do you have a preference?" with confidence as if they're going to choose one of those two options.

If the client needs more information on the company quoted, take the time to answer their questions and reassure them.

If the client objects, you can use the scripts outlined below to move them over the line. If the client is on board, start taking the application.

Remember, prospects don't usually think it over. If they say they need to think it over, it's because you gave an unconvincing presentation.

If you gave a great presentation, there won't be any objections.

> *"Now, the final step is very simple. We just need gather the remaining information to complete the application and to set up a convenient time to have a nurse come out to complete the medical exam."*

Then you can complete the application and move them to the next stage of your process.

Assumptive Selling

This script is similar to the consultative script, but frames the conversation a little differently.

> *"Hi Bill, this is Agent Schrader calling from DEA Insurance—how are you doing today? Did I catch you at a bad time?"*

Again, you value their time by asking the initial question, but most people will say no to the second part.

Move on to your purpose:

> *"Great, the purpose of my call is to make sure we understand the purchase you want to make, to make sure we are quoting you with the appropriate carriers—and to coordinate the rest of the process of applying."*

You are assuming the sale already, since they reached out to you.

Outline who you are:

> *"As you may already know, DEA Insurance is a life insurance comparison service, we are not an insurance company and not owned by an insurance company. We gather your information to provide free life insurance quotes with top companies like MetLife, Prudential, Banner Life, SBLI and John Hancock to name a few. This gives us the ability to be unbiased in our offerings to you the consumer. First off, were there any questions you had for me?"*

This breaks down any walls and establishes you as trustworthy.

Next, you establish the need:

> *"Was this new policy to replace an existing policy? In addition to? Who's the beneficiary? What made you get online to quote a new policy?"*

Keep asking questions. Establish multiple reasons the client needs life insurance, and take notes. Establishing the need will cement the sale, and from this point you can close it out much like the consultative script. When you get to the actual sale, though, you have them book in a specific time for their exam:

> *"Now we have decided on a preliminary policy, let's take a look at the calendar. I have [date] available, what time works for you?"*

This ensures you get the final follow-through and don't lose the sale at the last moment.

Now, you don't have to use these exact scripts. If you want to, you can adjust them for your personality and approach, but these are good frameworks to start with. These are the scripts we use, and we've made thousands of sales with them.

How To Run The Call

It's critical that **you** run the call. You need to direct the flow of the conversation, without letting the customer barrage you with questions.

Sure—you can answer their questions, but you need to command the process and stick to the script outline. If it seems daunting, here's exactly what you say when someone starts peppering you with questions:

> *"Those are great questions, and we'll get to those in just a moment. Before we dive into that, I want to give you an idea of who I am and how I work.*

*You see, I don't work on behalf of any life insurance company—I work on behalf of my customers. I represent over 50 life insurance companies to my customers, so the purpose of this call is to understand **you**. That way I can shop the market effectively and get you the perfect type of coverage for your situation."*

You need to get that out before you answer any of their questions—otherwise, they can just hang up on you after draining you of all the information they wanted.

To do this effectively, you need to create a powerful presence on the phone. You need to speak confidently. For me, standing up and walking around while I'm talking really helps me to sound confident and purposeful. Standing up improves your posture and breathing, which allows you to project your voice and sound more confident and in control.

You also want to project warmth throughout the conversation. When you ask them what prompted them to buy life insurance, acknowledge and relate to their reason.

If they say they have two kids and want to make sure they're taken care of, ask about the kids, and come back to them a few times throughout the conversation as you make your point:

"This is going to protect Rosie and Cameron if anything were to happen to you."

Keep it about them. Relate everything you talk about to their core motivation, and reassure them they're making an admirable, wise decision.

The Importance of Your Database

There is one mistake nearly all life insurance agents make, and it drastically slows down the growth of their business.

When they are selling over the phone, they want to get a 'yes' from the customer and an instant sale. A lot of the time, though, they hear...

> *"You know, it's just not the right time at the moment—*
> *can you call me in a few months?"*

... And they never follow up with that person again.

It's critical you do follow up with them. Set a reminder in your CRM and contact them in a few months. Remember—they don't really know you, so it's not all that surprising they don't want to commit to a big purchase right away. But if you are in touch every few months, they will get to know you, and when they're ready to make their purchase, you'll be the only person they want to talk to about it.

I've been doing this for over a decade now, and here's what I've learned:

If they say they're not ready right now, ask them why. It might be price, it might be the product, it might be a lack of trust. Once you have an answer, you can set a follow up. Follow up with people even if you don't quote them anything on your initial call.

It's really powerful to be able to come to your desk every morning and have leads to contact who asked you weeks or months ago to follow up with them. These are really good leads that can become a huge source of sales—and they require less work than completely new leads too.

Yes, it's great to get sales right now. But take a long view here— if you don't get the sale today, it will be easier for you to get it in a few months. Most of the time people say no, it's a smokescreen.

Remember: they don't know you. They filled out a form on a website (which probably didn't have your name on it), so on first contact, they're trying to figure you out. They're trying to establish whether you're trustworthy, whether your offer is any good, and whether you're the right person to help them.

If you follow up with them a few times, send them an email or two with your photo and license number in the signature, and your contact information, you can build trust over time.

eApps

Regardless of whether the lead converts on the first call or the tenth, after you make the sale, you need to take the application.

The old-school way of doing it is to...

- Get the 25+ page document from the insurance company.

- Fill it out and scan, fax or mail it to the customer.

- Have them sign it and send it back to you.

You are not going to be doing that any more.

These days, we have technology that allows us to do online applications and get electronic signatures instantly.

There are a couple of different ways to do this.

IGO eApp

Most uplines and MGAs will give you access to an app called the IGO eApp by iPipeline. IGO just means the application is placed "In Good Order"—it's got all the information necessary, with nothing missing.

The only problem with iGo eApp is that they don't have all the major companies on their platform, and it's a little slow. You're entering every piece of information into the system, and the system needs to recognize it before you can proceed. It usually takes anywhere from 15 to 25 minutes to complete an eApp over the phone. However, once it's done, the application is complete and all you have to do is wait for approval.

Carrier Drop Ticket

This comes from the life insurance companies directly. This system allows you to just submit a ticket (with the name, address, phone number, email, SSN, beneficiary information and driver's license), then the company's customer support team will contact the customer and schedule the exam for them.

The good thing about this is that your processing time is very short—only a few minutes. Then you just tell the client the company will be in touch to handle the rest of the process.

The bad thing about this is that you hand control over to a call center. They probably don't care as much as you do about this client, and the client then has time to change their mind. You also just have to hope the call center rep knows what they are doing, and doesn't mess up your sale—assuming they ever get hold of the client.

When you submit a carrier drop ticket, the carrier also orders the medical exam and get the medical records. So, if you decide to take your customer's application elsewhere (for example, if they got an AOTA response from this carrier at a higher price), you can't use the exam or those medical records. The initial company paid for it all, so they're not going to give all the data up to another life insurance company.

Then your client has to take another medical exam, get more copies of their records, and that's going to take *another* four to six weeks to process.

So, if you think there's a chance of pivoting to a new carrier, this is not the right system to use.

Finally, there is one more option (and I think this is the best of both worlds). There are not a lot of these out there, but they're consistently growing in number.

MGA Drop Ticket

An MGA Drop Ticket is a platform where your upline creates their own drop ticket. It's got the same information as the carrier drop ticket, except that they order the medical exam and the medical records. They have full control of all the data, in case you want to pivot to a different life insurance company for this particular customer.

The downside to this is that you take a little less compensation—usually five to ten percent less than you would get on the 'open market'. However, you don't have to do any processing whatsoever.

With iGo eApp and Carrier Drop Ticket, you're also managing the underwriting process. If something comes up during underwriting (say, the company needs a financial statement or scuba diving questionnaire), you have to take care of it.

With the MGA Drop Ticket, your upline will have case managers who handle all of those ongoing details. You don't have to think about it again until it comes out at the offer stage. It's like having a team of assistants to take care of all the finicky details for you, so you can just focus on sales and marketing.

It can be hard to get your head around why you would take *less* compensation. But look at it this way: you are removing all the non-revenue producing tasks from your daily workflow.

All the time and attention that would usually go into handling the underwriting process can now be channeled into making more sales—which in turn creates more compensation.

When I first started using the MGA Drop Ticket system, it created a huge breakthrough in my business. Anyone who is doing all their selling over the phone should absolutely be using MGA Drop Tickets.

Those extra five to ten points are nothing compared to the numbers you can bring in when you just focus on sales and marketing.

Lists of MGA Drop Ticket providers can be found at selltermlife.com/book-resources.

PART 2

HOW TO BUILD A SALES AND MARKETING MACHINE

CHAPTER 5

Create a Sales Machine

Here's the hard truth: if you're not calling a new lead within the first five minutes of them hitting your system, you're leaving money on the table. The sooner you contact them, the more likely you are to win their business.

Contacting a lead right after they've filled out a form achieves a number of things:

First, you're making an excellent first impression. Most customers will be surprised about how quick you were to call them. This is an immediate icebreaker and creates some goodwill towards you.

You'll also get to speak to the customer while they're in an ideal position—still in front of the computer in "buying mode." They haven't had the opportunity to switch gears. Life insurance is still very much top of mind for them.

Finally, you'll often catch them before they've explored the competition.

Now, no one wants to be glued to their email all for the entire workday to catch each new leads right away.

Fortunately, this process can be completely automated.

If you spend a little time putting the systems in place, you can always be notified the moment a new lead comes in. There are plenty of software options available that allow you to set up text or email notifications to notify you of a lead. Some phone systems will even auto-dial the lead as soon as you pick up the phone.

It's key to take advantage of technology like this. It makes your processes more efficient, frees up your time and reduces your stress and mental overhead. In the long run, all those things combined mean you'll be able to make more sales and get greater enjoyment out of your work.

CRM Selection

All CRMs (customer relationship managers) are not created equal. The vast majority of CRMs available have little to differentiate them from each other. They all integrate the same technology with only small differences to set them apart.

Most life insurance agents use their CRM as a tool to input client details, take notes on calls, and store information for future use. But a good CRM with sales automation capabilities can be so much more than an administrative tool.

Your CRM should be your ultimate sales machine.

The most efficient way to work leads is to harness the full power of your CRM. By creating workflows (automated processes within the CRM), you'll be able to create real momentum in your business that would just not be possible if you were to do it all manually.

Workflow Implementation

Your CRM should allow for a customizable workflow that self-manages your priorities. We call this a queue-based or list-based selling platform.

Here's how it works:

1. When a new lead enters your system, it pops up in your CRM so you can contact them immediately.

2. You make the phone call, then enter the end result once the call is completed (contacted, quoted, not interested etc.).

3. The CRM files the previous lead away, and presents the next best lead automatically based on the rules of the system.

4. The lead you just called will come back in your queue automatically at the time you specified. ie. in three hours, one day, two days etc.

That's all there is to it. You shouldn't be spending time and energy deciding who to call next. Your CRM system should serve this information to *you*.

CRMs keep getting better as new technology comes out. We'll have a list of recommended CRMs that can handle these queue or list based selling platforms at selltermlife.com/book-resources. We'll also have a document available with the workflows our agency uses that you can use as a baseline. Simply hand this document over to the CRM of your choice and pay the CRM you choose to build it out.

Application of the Platform

Using your CRM in this way allows you to design a standard daily workflow exactly to your specifications.

When you show up to the office in the morning, you'll be presented with the best lead to call. Throughout the day, you'll be able to call and sell your leads, just by clicking through the list your CRM presents to you. Each contact in your workflow will show up automatically when it's the right time for you to call them.

When you've completed your queue of leads for the day, you can move on to other parts of the business (and I always recommend working on your marketing, so you maintain a steady flow of leads coming in).

This is really all it takes to manage your leads.

Another core use of the platform is tracking the number of times each lead has been contacted—most people will need as many as 12 points of contact with you before they buy. I do this over a period of 45 days, but you can set up your system to coordinate any number of calls over another length of time.

Managing call frequency ensures you're maximizing your chances of closing each potential customer. If they have stopped responding to calls or emails, your system already knows when to automatically close that lead.

You can operate with the confidence that every lead is being called the right number of times at the right time, every time.

Today, fewer than 10% of life insurance agents are using a CRM with the right infrastructure to handle custom workflows. It's really key you invest in a CRM that can deploy this sales process for you. With the time and availability a CRM sales machine opens up, you'll have the necessary mental space to focus on the marketing that really grows your business.

Platform Ownership

Your website is the hub for all you do. But if you don't own your hub, you don't control the machine your entire business depends on.

When it comes to creating a website, most agents outsource the job to a website service and pay a monthly subscription for their made-to-order site. But this means that if you stop paying for the site, it's no longer yours—it's the developer's. And if you don't have the source code (the most permanent form of all your website's code), then you don't truly have ownership.

If you're not in control of your site, you're not in control of your marketing machine.

New software is coming out all the time, and you need to be able to implement it. Otherwise, you're not harnessing your site's most important function—generating *all* your leads.

Using your website as a complete hub is what allows you the flexibility to work as you please on your business. Owning the platform creates location independence and time freedom.

More Information, More Trust

I've emphasised the importance of trust in establishing the kind of rapport that leads to sales.

One of the most crucial areas of your website is the About Page. This page can easily increase the prospect's trust and familiarity with you, and will be one of the most highly trafficked pages on your entire site.

Visitors should get the sense of a real person with a life, a history, a family—it makes you real and relatable. Pictures can truly be worth a thousand words here.

Sending leads a link to your About Page can play a huge role in conversions. Once they've encountered you as a real person, leads are more likely to click through the rest of your site and see what you're all about.

These days, people of all ages are online. Everyone is within arm's reach of their smartphone all the time, so having all your information accessible online is an incredibly powerful tool.

People can check you out in their own time, while they're waiting for lunch, getting coffee, *or* at the exact moment they need to buy some life insurance.

This is a huge opportunity. Not only can you be right in front of them at the moment they make the crucial decision, you can follow up with them and make them the right offers at the right time.

It's a massive advantage over the agents who are still doing all their business in person—there's just no way they can have that kind of presence.

Lead Building

In order to build your own marketing machine and have longevity in this business, you *must* be generating your own leads.

Many agents get into a bad habit of buying all their leads, instead of building their own acquisition channels. This can be a volatile practice for a couple of reasons:

- A lead vendor's quality can go down at any moment (vendors sometimes implement a new marketing strategy that crushes the quality of their leads).

- Any lead source with a good enough ROI is bound to be figured out. Call centers will get wind of a good source, and simply buy out all the leads—leaving you high and dry.

I've seen this second problem occur more than once. Even small boutique lead vendors get bought out by big call centers because they can generate such good leads. This speaks to the biggest issue with this system:

There is a cap to the quality of leads that vendors can generate before someone tries to buy them out.

Buying your leads means depending on someone else for their quality and availability, which leaves you with zero control over the most critical element of your business. You must have the ability to generate your own high-quality leads.

I'll cover more on building this marketing machine and lead platform in later chapters. For now, you should understand that it all comes down to owning and optimizing your website in order to attract and convert your leads.

Website Conversion

Many agent websites out there get traffic, but very few leads. They just don't convert well.

A quick note here on some of this lingo:

> *A 'conversion' happens any time a visitor to your website takes an action you want them to. It might be filling out a quote form, booking a call with you, or signing up for more information from your email list—an action that takes them from being a visitor to being a lead. When I say a site doesn't convert well, I just mean that most of the visitors coming to the site do not take the desired action that makes them into a real lead.*

Most of the life insurance agents who go out of business do so because of this issue. They're getting traffic to their site, but maybe only half the number of leads they need to survive.

If your business is going to stay afloat online, your website needs to convert well.

When I first started my website five years ago, I was was getting decent traffic. For every 100 visitors, I was getting two forms filled out—a 2% conversion rate. I kept chugging along like this until I read some articles on conversion optimization. I switched a few things up and was soon getting three leads per 100 visitors.

Today I've built up my website quite a bit more. On average, the website now generates five to eight leads per 100 visitors at any given time.

A poorly converting website can truly break a business. You work so hard to bring in the traffic, but your website may be the reason why your leads aren't inquiring with you. But with some specific design elements and carefully written content, your lead count can double, even triple, and create some serious momentum in your business.

Design to Convert

I'll say it again: your website *must* be built to convert visitors to leads.

If your site is getting traffic but you're not converting 5% or more of those visitors into leads, you should look into redesigning it (or at least changing a few key factors).

However, be cautious when using website agencies. Compared to the businesses they're used to designing for, life insurance is a different animal.

Working in life insurance is about selling an intangible product to a consumer, based solely on emotion.

The website needs to make an emotional impact, especially with images. Cheesy stock photos won't do it—they'll just put people off. A visitor need to see photos that evoke real emotion.

Similarly, calls to action must be centered around life insurance itself, not just "get quotes." I see too many agent websites that could be generating a lot more leads than they are, just because the copy isn't specific and compelling.

Tips for Better Website Conversion

Some key things to include on your website to ensure better conversion:

1. Instant quotes that collect contact information

   - Make sure you have a "display quotes" option on your call to action button.
   - NinjaQuoter.com is the best software available to do this right now.

2. Intentional images and copy

   - Choose images that evoke emotion.
   - Copy must be centered around benefits of buying life insurance, *not* about what an excellent agent you are.

3. Fast website load times

   - Slow websites are proven to cause visitors to leave the site before engaging.
   - A website that doesn't load within five seconds will cause more than 75% of visitors leave immediately.

4. Scrolling/floating quoter

   - Call to action button needs to be front and center all the time, moving with the user as they're reading and scrolling.
   - "Display quotes" button should be the brightest thing on the page.

These steps are critical to the conversion rate of your business. We've helped hundreds of agents implement these processes, so if you'd like us to do the same for you, go to selltermlife.com/website-offer and we'll get it moving.

Think of conversion optimization as the basis from which you'll grow your business. In the next chapters, we're going to delve into how to build your online marketing strategy. As you scale up the number of people coming to your site, you'll want to make sure you're capturing as many of them as leads as possible.

CHAPTER 6

Build a Marketing Strategy

Marketing is the single most important thing you can do to grow your online business. Like I mentioned earlier, think of marketing as part of your prospecting efforts, just in a new medium. Learning about marketing and developing the right strategies for your business is *not* taking away from your lead generation time—it's going to make it more efficient.

To lay out an effective marketing plan, you must first be able to answer some critical questions.

Most importantly: who are you marketing to?

Where do you have an edge? What are your interests? Who do you connect with best of all the kinds of people you speak to?

For example, if you love scuba diving, why not focus on selling life insurance to other scuba divers? You have a common interest, you have a reason to connect, you speak their language.

You *get* why they love scuba diving, and want to help them enjoy it even more by giving them peace of mind.

If you're targeting business owners or executives, you need to really know the demographic. Find out where they spend their time online, who they are paying attention to, and how to present an offer to them so it's a total 'no-brainer' for them to buy it.

Regardless of what niche you go after, it really helps to have a personal connection to it and to build a deep understanding of those customers before you try to sell them anything.

Alternately, you can filter your potential customers by the kind of products you want to sell. Many products are built for specific market segments, such as...

- Federal employees
- Seniors
- Diabetics

Find the products in the market that allow you to differentiate yourself. This is a competitive industry, so you need to give yourself as much of an advantage as possible. Having something specific to discuss with potential customers gives you a real edge over other agents.

If you're great at selling term life insurance and final expense coverage, stick to those products. Don't get into selling cash-value life insurance or other products if you're not good at it.

Even if you can generate leads for your weaker product areas, it doesn't mean you have the competitive edge you need. Play to your strengths.

Once you know who you want to market to, you need to work out how much you can spend to do it. Your marketing budget will determine how you go about the entire process.

You either have more time than money, or more money than time.

Once you pick who you're going to market to, pick one or two of the marketing concepts later in this chapter, and execute them daily, according to your budget and schedule.

Pick a Niche and be Unique

Agents get the best traction online (and even offline) when they pick a niche. Focus on one specific area, and become the go-to agent for people in that demographic.

For example, maybe you know a lot about getting coverage for diabetics. Build a website that is *just* designed around getting life insurance for people with diabetes. Don't address anything else— really laser target people in your chosen demographic.

There are two key advantages to this:

1. Your site will rank faster and higher for your specific terms in the search engines when it specifically addresses a common search query (in this example, 'life insurance for diabetics').

2. It opens up a lot of profitable marketing channels you can't use by being a "generalist".

This is where agents are quickly getting leads and generating the most income. They are picking a niche, focusing on a few marketing concepts, and doubling down until they really own their niche. Once you've got it locked down, you can duplicate the process in a new niche.

This approach opens up a lot of opportunities you won't ever see if you take a general approach. You can go to trade shows, sponsor events, get on niche podcasts... It's the biggest opportunity for agents who are starting out to get some real traction in their new business.

Not only are the opportunities huge, but focusing on a niche will make it *much* easier for you to apply all of the marketing concepts we'll be focusing on in the next part of the book.

Importance of Niche Selection

After you've been running an internet life insurance business for a while, you'll recognize that there are some prospects who are simply more trouble than they're worth. On the other hand, there are some fantastic prospects who are highly likely to convert, and those are the ones you want to target.

There are literally hundreds—maybe even thousands—of untapped niches in life insurance.

By untapped, I mean there's no go-to resource with an agent servicing this niche. The fastest growing internet life insurance businesses I've seen are all focused on a specific niche. These specialists tend to have more stable internet life insurance businesses than the generalists who write coverage for everyone.

Why?

There are just so many niche marketing opportunities that you can't leverage as a generalist. There's nothing wrong with being a generalist per se, but it's very hard to set yourself apart from all the other life insurance agents out there. What makes you unique besides being independent, and offering access to all of the top-rated carriers in the market?

This lack of differentiation can really slow the growth of your business, and makes you less focused and effective in your marketing efforts.

We're going to break this down into three sections. The first section will be niche selection—how to go about finding the right niche or niches. Then we'll go into how to build out your USP, or unique selling proposition. Finally, we'll get into how to market to your chosen niche, building off of your USP and unique experience.

Find the Right Niche

Selecting the niche you want to target is one of the most important early decisions you'll make in your business. Don't worry, though—you can always go after multiple niches, or even switch niches later on. Just start with one you know you can do an excellent job for, and then you can expand when you're ready.

Niching down to a smaller group of life insurance prospects allows you to serve that market segment extremely well—'super-serving' them, if you will.

Pick a niche you already know something about. Perhaps you could leverage knowledge you've gained from one of your hobbies, a condition you or a family member has experienced, or a tough case you've placed previously. Maybe you already know several people in this niche you can ask for feedback, advice, or even introductions.

The key is simply to have a working knowledge of your niche before you try to serve them. If you pick a niche you know nothing about, you're prone to make a lot of rookie mistakes.

Pick a Stable and/or Growing Niche

Specific health conditions, such as diabetes or depression, provide very stable niches. There are hundreds of different health conditions you could work with, or if you prefer, you could also target groups of people like small business owners or federal employees.

These niches are 'evergreen'—they will always be around—and there are plenty of businesses outside of life insurance that cater to them. You can partner up with those external businesses to generate targeted traffic for your website and create a mutually beneficial relationship.

Some growing niches, at least at the time of writing, include seniors, e-cigarette users, medical marijuana users and the no-exam life insurance market. There are always going to be expanding markets, so keep an eye on what's happening in your community and across the country to be able to make the most of that growth.

Just make sure you don't pick a niche that is too small or too hard to help. For example, rock climbers in the US make up a very small niche. There's definitely a need, but there are not enough climbers for you to target to make it worthwhile. That might be a secondary niche you service, in combination with a bigger market segment.

To get started, I would make a list of all the niches you have a working knowledge of, and decide which one has the biggest potential. Then you need to create your Unique Selling Proposition, or USP.

Create a Unique Selling Proposition

After you've identified your target market, the next step is to determine what will make you stand out from all the other life insurance agents serving the same niche. This is your Unique Selling Proposition, or USP, which answers one simple question: *why would your customers buy from you instead of your competitors?*

Most life insurance websites don't have a unique selling proposition. They all say they'll get the best rates for their customers... but it's not unique, because every agent says it. Once a customer has seen the same promise on a few sites, it becomes empty and unbelievable.

Your Unique Selling Proposition is a promise to your customers about what they can expect from your business and its products and services.

You have to determine what unique features and benefits you can offer to your prospects your competitors can't, and then present that to them in an appealing way.

The best way to develop your USP is by talking to your potential customers. Listen to their complaints about the space you're in, or negative experiences they've previously had trying to get coverage, then turn that frustration into your Unique Selling Proposition.

For example, if you were to serve the diabetic niche, what would your customers say is their biggest pain is in obtaining life insurance? Do they feel judged by every agent they speak to? Are they promised great coverage and then get AOTA responses every time? What would be a unique approach in that situation?

For example, if you're a diabetic yourself, you'll be able to relate to your prospects as part of your USP. You could say something along the lines of *"diabetics helping other diabetics understand and find the best life insurance rates".*

In this instance you're showing prospects that you understand their situation, their concerns and their fears. You *have* diabetes and can help them through this process.

Or if you're not diabetic, you could be the agent who secures life insurance for diabetics with no medical exam. Many diabetics don't like exams, so that's another USP you could use.

You also want to provide your niche more value or unique benefits than your competition can offer. It could be through expertise, experience, technology, or maybe access to a product most agents don't sell.

If you can't come up with a Unique Selling Proposition for the niche you're focused on, then it's probably not the right niche.

You *must* be unique and offer something other agents don't, so when you get prospects on the phone, you'll have an edge over everyone else.

When you come up with your Unique Selling Proposition, it should be displayed prominently on your website and all throughout your marketing. Everyone you deal with should immediately see and understand your USP.

Once you have your niche and USP, it's time to launch into marketing... and this is where most agents get stuck.

How to Market to a Niche

Most agents build a website and think people will just find them. I like to compare it to the movie, *Field of Dreams*, where agents are hearing the same voice Kevin Costner hears:

"If you will build, they will come."

Unfortunately, that's completely false in this business. They won't come just because you built it.

Building an internet life insurance agency is not the entrepreneurial version of *Field of Dreams*.

You have to do much more than just 'build it' if you want customers to start coming in.

When you build a brick-and-mortar business on a street corner, or in a crowded shopping mall, customers will naturally wander into your store because they're nearby and see your sign. When you start an internet business, it's like having a store with no signage and no lights on. Shoppers won't even realize you're there.

People won't just stumble upon your website and request a quote from you. You have to actively persuade potential customers to come to your store and to buy your life insurance products... but how do you do this?

You identify different marketing channels and create a marketing plan.

Ideally you'll have three or more sources of traffic. Some agents live nicely off one source of traffic, but I strongly recommend against it.

Online marketing channels are volatile. Their performance changes all the time. Google might change their algorithm, a competing channel might hit the market, or some big event could change how consumers interact with the channel. Relying on a single source that could be taken away from you at any time is unwise.

Here are some ways successful internet life insurance agents are getting in front of their niche:

Create the <u>ultimate</u> resource for life insurance in this niche as a website.

Let's say you're going to target chronic obstructive pulmonary disease (COPD). You can create a "pillar article" explaining in-depth what to expect when searching for life insurance with COPD, and refers to supporting articles with extra information. Things like:

- *"How ABC Life Insurance Underwrites COPD."* Create this for every company—potentially 25+ unique articles to establish your authority.

- *"How [COPD Medication Name] Affects Life Insurance Rates"*—potentially 10+ articles.

- *"Securing [Term, Universal, Whole Life, Final Expense] life insurance with COPD"*—at least four articles.

- "Top Five Life Insurance Companies to Consider with COPD."

- "How To Get Coverage with NO Exam with COPD."

By creating the ultimate online resource, you'll begin to rank in the search engines for every conceivable variation of COPD and life insurance. Then other COPD sites will naturally start linking to your site, sending referral traffic and boosting your search engine presence.

You're probably thinking, *"I don't know all this information for the niche I'm thinking of!"*

That's perfectly normal. You just have to treat this as a research project: get all the facts and articulate them onto a website. This will make you the expert and set you leagues ahead of your competitors.

Make a list of the Top 100 websites in your niche you can leverage.

You're going to create a spreadsheet of all the potential websites where you could advertise, write a guest post, get mentioned on their social media or featured in their email list.

On your spreadsheet, include the business name, website URL, primary contact name (if any), phone number, email, Facebook and Twitter accounts.

Then you want to rank the list by potential impact. Add a "Facebook Like Count" column or "Alexa Rating" and sort your top opportunities by those numbers.

Just visit their Facebook Pages and record how many "likes" they have, or go to Alexa.com, enter their URL and put in their ranking.

Even the smallest niche website can bring you business—this is just to give you a general ranking of your opportunities. Once your authority website is finished, you're going to do some outreach.

Get on Google and look for blogs and websites. See if there are any directories within the niche you're focusing on. Go to non-profit or association websites and see who sponsors them.

Find those Top 100 websites and build a marketing plan around them.

In no particular order, here are some ways to build this plan:

1. If they have advertising on their site, ask for a media kit so you can assess if that would be a worthwhile investment.

2. If they have a blog, ask to write an article for their audience about securing life insurance for their niche.

3. If they have an email list or newsletter, ask them what it would take to advertise on that list.

4. If they have a 'resources' section on their site, ask them to review your website and services, and ask for a placement in that section.

5. If they have a Facebook following, ask to review your services and share with their audience.

6. Take all the Facebook pages and run Facebook Ads to those audiences (we'll discuss how to do this in a future chapter).

7. Find out where your niche's next events are and buy a booth, then go and meet your prospects in person.

8. Participate in your niche's forums. Making sure you add value before ever pitching your product, or buy advertising on those forums.

9. If there are podcasts, get on as a guest to talk about your niche and services.

These ideas are just scraping the surface of what's possible.

There are many other ways to get targeted traffic to your website, and I recommend you regularly test out new customer acquisition channels and advertising strategies.

Once you've found something that works, do everything you can to maximize the flow of new customers through the traffic stream. Whether it's through an increase in your advertising spend, or publishing more content to the platform, double down on it.

Move all your marketing dollars to what's working.

In most cases, it takes money to advertise. If you don't have the money for it, focus on creating your ultimate guide, guest posting on blogs and participating in forums. The results will be slower, but you will be building your authority in your niche and gradually building momentum for your business.

Picking a niche makes every other part of your business easier.

Take a niche, nail down your USP so you can differentiate yourself and confirm you have an upper hand in the niche, and then test different marketing channels.

Once you find a marketing funnel that's consistently profitable, you're in business. Once you've mastered these marketing skills, you can try it on other niches and expand your business as often as you want.

I'll leave this section with this:

> Jack Welch (the famous CEO of General Electric, or GE) had an unusual approach to markets, considering how big General Electric was when he was running it.
>
> GE was active in multiple markets, including home appliances, mechanics, finances, food, and even nuclear energy.

Welch treated every GE unit as its own separate entity, and rolled out a very simple rule to determine which units would be continued or not:

Can we be Number One or Number Two in this market?

If GE could take one of the top spots, they would invest all the necessary resources to make it happen. If they couldn't hold one of those positions, they would shut down the unit and focus on the profitable markets.

This is a powerful way to look at your chosen niche. Focus on what's profitable and cut everything else.

PART 3

INTERNET MARKETING
FOR
LIFE INSURANCE SALES

CHAPTER 7

Buying Leads

While I recommend owning your lead platform and generating your own leads, during your first year it's inevitable that you're going to have to buy some leads.

Once you've built your platform, picked your niche, and started implementing your marketing plan, it's still going to take time for leads to start flowing into your business.

It's critical you build up some experience on the phones while you're waiting for your lead machine to come to life.

Unless you still have a job while you're building your online business, you're also going to need to make some money. You need to live, after all, and there's nothing wrong with buying some quality leads to tide you over until your business is humming by itself.

The time it will take for your lead platform to start working really depends on how much marketing you're doing. If you're learning proactively for three or four hours day, applying everything you find, and really double down on a handful of marketing channels, you can expect leads to start coming in consistently within six months.

If you can't commit that kind of time, and only have a couple of hours every other day, it's probably going to take a year before you start getting enough leads to support yourself.

It all depends on your commitment to your marketing plan and how much time you can spend on it each day. If you manage to build a lead flow quickly, you'll probably want to supplement the numbers to really give yourself some runway.

Regardless of your current situation, you should start buying leads so that you can start practicing selling over the phone.

Selling online is a different game to selling in person. You need to work much harder to create rapport and trust, so you might as well cut your teeth on someone else's leads, rather than leads you've worked hard to bring in.

When I started buying life insurance leads in 2007, they were exclusive leads that cost roughly $25 per lead. I was pretty new to selling over the phone, but I was able to start making a good living because lead quality was so good. Unfortunately in 2009, the lead quality plummeted overnight.

At the time, a new ping posting technology was created, causing the plunge in quality. A new lead would be generated on a website and routed to their main lead buyer, then pinged out to other vendors and sold again.

Leads were no longer exclusive, so the poor customer might have five or six agents call them in a day. Unfortunately, many lead vendors today are still using this technology, which means the lead quality from most of the big players is absolutely terrible.

The only way to win those leads is to be the very first agent to call them, which means you have to be permanently attached to your computer, ready to dial them the very second the lead hits your inbox. **It's an exhausting, stressful and frustrating way to get customers.**

That's why you have to start generating your own leads if you want to make it work for the long-term in this business. As I said though, it takes time, so let's dig into some of the ways you can buy good quality leads when you're starting out.

Remember that in this industry, you are a small fish in a big pond. You are competing with call centers and big agencies. If a lead source is creating a great ROI, you should expect one of the big players to snap it up as soon as they catch wind of it.

The best leads will all go this way: a boutique lead vendor will enter the market with premium leads, and then overnight they're gone. They get bought out by the insurance companies and agencies, so if you hit it big with a great lead source, just remember you can't depend on it.

Get as much out of it as you possibly can while it's still available, and then be ready to move on when the well dries up.

Get Licensed Nationally

If you are licensed to sell life insurance in all 50 states, you can go to the lead companies and negotiate a discount on their typical lead prices. You'll get access to leads from all over the country at a significantly cheaper rate than if you approached each state individually.

Most agents are buying locally or in a few states which drives up the cost of generating a lead. If you're able to take the "overflow" leads, you can negotiate a much better rate.

Lead companies can also generate leads cheaper for you without geo-targeting (finding out exactly where in the country the leads are coming from, which is necessary when you are only licensed in certain states).

Take on High-Risk Leads

I often see agents filter out high-risk leads because they aren't easy slam-dunk customers, but they are missing out on a huge opportunity by doing this.

First of all, because agents aren't as inclined to call high-risk leads, the prospects aren't getting inundated with calls from other agents. Second of all, high-risk individuals typically have higher premiums, resulting in higher commissions. Lastly, high-risk leads are cheaper than regular leads. I remember buying high-risk leads from a lead vendor at $4 a pop (in bulk) years ago. Even though I was only selling one in 25 leads or so, the numbers worked. The acquisition cost came out to about $100, but the premiums were huge!

And if you're bilingual, this is an even bigger opportunity. The Spanish-speaking market is absolutely massive here in the U.S., but the language barrier makes it even more difficult for high-risk consumers to get coverage.

Seek out Revenue Share Opportunities

Find websites that are generating leads and instead of selling the leads for, say, $15 per lead to a lead vendor or an affiliate offer, contact the owners and negotiate a revenue share. I've been successful with this several times. I came across a site that was generating good leads, I went through their quote path, and found they were selling the leads off to one of the big aggregators.

I got in contact with them, and said, *"Hey. Why don't you send these leads to us? We'll work them for you, and we'll pay you $XX if you want to get licensed."*

They got licensed, and because they were doing such a big volume, it would end up being a pretty hefty revenue share. There was no acquisition cost to me, I got half the comp, and it was great because there was no financial risk to me.

Search for Underground Lead Companies

There are numerous niche lead generation companies out there. They pop up all the time, as marketers rise through the ranks, generating leads with new technology we've never seen before.

These smaller agencies may not even specialize in life insurance leads. They might just be a marketing company or a lead generation company, but you can often contact them and see what they can turn up in the life insurance space.

There are lead companies you've never heard of that agents are doing *really* well with, and you won't ever hear about them because the agents don't tell anyone else about them. These agencies are out there, but it's only a matter of time before a bigger company acquires them.

Don't Ignore Aged Leads

Aged life insurance leads work. These leads may be a couple of weeks old, and even up to 90 days old. *(The Telephone Consumer Protection Act law requires you to contact a lead within 90 days of them filling in a form online.)*

For the agent who is willing to get on a dialer, there's money to be made. This is basically data mining. You load thousands of leads into the dialer, which can often call up to three numbers at once, and churn through the list of leads until you get some hits.

Buy 3,000 or 4,000 aged leads at a time. You can get through about 500 to 750 calls in a four-hour dialer session, probably quote three to five people, and make at least one sale in each session.

Admittedly, it takes a certain type of agent to do this. You must be patient, resilient and persistent. It takes time and grit, so I don't recommend aged leads unless you want to get trained quickly on selling over the phone, have a very low budget, or are already exceptional at closing people over the phone.

This is how I built my business when I first went out on my own. I bought 5000 to 6000 aged leads per month, and called them for four or five hours every day while I learned marketing. It was hard, but I did well with them. Most agents give up when they hear "no" too many times, but one "yes" is all you need to get some momentum.

Aged leads are also a great backstop. You can use them as a supplement, when things are slow, to get started, or as your main source. You just have to be committed, and recognize that it's all a numbers game.

Lead Buying Pooling

Money talks. The more leads you buy, the less they cost. There are groups of agents all over the country who pool their lead budgets so that they get a lower per-lead cost. If you are connected with a few agents who are selling over the phone and buying from the same lead source, you can try joining together to get a better deal from your vendors.

Buy According to the State Lead Volume

Most agents are licensed in the top 25 most populated states and buy their leads within those areas. There are another 10 to 15 less populated states that are completely underserved, so get licensed in those states and buy shared leads there.

The leads are less expensive than exclusive leads, and they're shared among far fewer agents, simply because there are not as many licensed life insurance agents serving those states. Your lead flow might be slower, but the quality will be high, because there's just less competition for their business.

CHAPTER 8

Search Engine Optimization (SEO)

Search Engine Optimization ("SEO") is made up of strategies that can be used to increase the amount of visitors to your website through getting high placements in the search engines. When you do this well, you can draw *a lot* of consistent traffic to your website.

The best part of SEO? This traffic is free and the bar is set very low for life insurance agents. Put in some consistent effort using the knowledge we teach you in this chapter and you'll start getting prospects contacting you for life insurance.

Search engine generated life insurance leads are the holy grail of online marketing. They are the highest quality online leads you can get, and they come directly to you.

These are consumers actively researching life insurance online. They're already thinking about buying coverage, and have already entered the buying cycle. It's up to you to answer their questions and build trust through your website and writing.

The most successful life insurance agents are a resource to their target markets. They provide real value up front, before they even get the prospect on the phone, and so they start each conversation from a position of strength.

How to Get Prospects

The entire premise of search engine marketing is about getting prospects to come to you, by writing content that helps them toward their buying decision.

Your prospects have real problems and real questions. They're coming online to get the answers and reassurance they need to move forward with coverage. By writing helpful content, you trade free advice for your prospects' trust and attention—the most valuable assets you can get when prospecting.

If you present the information your prospects are looking for in a straightforward, accessible way, this positions you as the go-to resource in their minds. You become the person who solved their problem or answered their question, which generates an extraordinary amount of trust.

That's why writing quality content on your website is so important.

The act of writing is about producing assets. You are building a foundation of knowledge and insight that will produce long-term results. Writing is not a get rich quick scheme.

If you've written a helpful article and have a high-converting website, there's a very good chance the article will start generating warm leads for you. The more high-quality articles you have, the more leads you can expect.

Let's take a look at how to actually achieve this.

Step #1: Write What You Know

Every day, thousands of new pieces of content are published online. It's a lot to compete with, which is why it's critical you're very intentional about the content you're producing. If you're going to spend the time writing articles on life insurance, make sure you have an edge.

Too many agents try to copy other agent's sites or write generic content that's been written over and over. This is boring, ineffective and a waste of time.

Creating content is about sharing your unique insights with your potential customers. The 'sweet spot' for building content that will generate leads is at the intersection of your particular knowledge and passions.

There are a lot of really experienced and knowledgeable life insurance agents out there. Those who stand out online leverage their specialized knowledge with a passion their audience can really relate to.

For some agents, the competitive edge in their content might be a product not many people have access to.

Case in point: I know an agent who markets a specific life insurance product to postal workers. The Postal Service deducts the cost of this product directly from their paycheck, so the agent closes an insane amount of business just by focusing on this one product.

In another example, a different agent is focused on the overweight and obese market segment. He has access to life insurance products that have no height or weight questions, and don't require a medical exam. It's no surprise his close rates are also extremely high.

Both those agents have a clear edge over their competition because of a product they have access to. Any content they write should be focused on those products, as well as addressing the hopes, fears, questions and concerns of the people who would benefit from the product.

Alternately, the competitive edge in your content could be an area of expertise or a common interest with your target market.

For example, you may be a scuba diver. This means you can speak the same language as other divers, can connect on various issues in the scuba diving world, and fully understand their motivations, fears and focuses.

Maybe you're ex-military and know SGLI, VGLI and other military benefits like the back of your hand. Maybe you know how to underwrite PTSD better than anyone, and can create a deep sense of familiarity and camaraderie that other veterans find reassuring.

In these examples, and in any other scenario where you're serving people you can relate to, your connection with your prospects will be much stronger than anything another agent could create. If your prospects understand you and can sense the shared focus, they'll be far more likely to trust you and believe you have their best interests at heart.

To attract those people to your site through the search engines, you want to build a list of 50 to 100 topics to write about.

I know it seems like a lot, but it's important to have a lot of content around your chosen subjects in order to rank in the search engines.

These 50 to 100 topics will be what's referred to by marketers as "long-tail keywords".

Long-Tail Keywords

Long-tail keywords are specific phrases that visitors are likely to type into the search engines when they are researching coverage or when they're getting close to making a buying decision.

Trying to rank for terms such as "term life insurance" or "whole life insurance" is too competitive. You'd be competing with the big insurance companies for those terms, not to mention you'd catch people at the beginning of their research, when they don't have a clear idea of what they're looking for.

The agents who see the most success with long-tail keywords are focusing on less competitive long-tail keywords. This is because the search terms tend to change as the prospect becomes more serious about buying life insurance.

A motivated life insurance prospect is going to search something like "buy $250,000 term life insurance policy with no exam".

Let's say you wanted to focus on scuba divers. Here's a sample list of 10 keywords you could use to create your content:

1. Life insurance for scuba divers (your pillar article).

2. Life insurance for scuba diving instructors.

3. What to do if you've been declined for life insurance because of scuba diving.

4. No-exam life insurance options for scuba divers.

5. How does scuba diving affect my life insurance rates?

6. Best life insurance companies for scuba divers.

7. What life insurance companies need to know about your scuba diving.

8. How depth of your dives affects your life insurance.

9. How penetration diving will affect your life insurance (proximity to caves, shipwrecks etc.).

10. What rescue divers need to know about life insurance.

You get the idea. Do this with at least five of your strengths or areas of expertise, and get to work on tackling the list.

These focused topics or "long tail keywords" will bring you the most qualified traffic to your website.

Step #2: Write Consistent, In-Depth Articles

To begin with, you want to be publishing three to four articles per week. Research each topic in depth, and make sure you create enough value that your visitors will really engage with the content. You want them to immediately see the value in working with you or your agency because your expertise on the subject is on display.

Best Practices for Writing Articles

1. Each article should be 1,000+ words. The longer the article, the better. Don't stuff articles with useless information—make sure everything is actually valuable (or at least interesting).

2. Internally link your similar articles together. For example, in the scuba diving scenario above, the articles should link to the "life insurance for scuba divers" article and the "life insurance for scuba divers article" should link back to most of those articles. This is really important, as it shows the search engine that your content is relevant to scuba divers looking for life insurance.

3. Include appealing, relatable images. Most visitors will quickly leave a page if they see plain text only. Use images that evoke some sort of emotion for your targeted group.

4. Put a call to action at the beginning and end of each article. Use something like "For instant life insurance quotes, fill out the form on the right and rates will be displayed immediately". A significant number of people won't even read the whole article and you'll still get the lead from the introduction.

5. Use bullet points, numerical lists and charts to break up the text when possible. Walls of text are off-putting and difficult to read, even for the most enthusiastic prospects. Make it easy for people to engage with your content.

The reason most agents don't get traffic or leads from the search engines is because they don't go to these extra lengths when writing.

If you can stick with this for six to nine months, you'll start getting inbound traffic. Your content needs to age in the search engines a bit, unless you can afford to promote it via paid traffic.

Treat it as a research paper where you want to provide all the facts to the person reading your article.

I have articles that have been generating daily leads from the search engines for the last five years. I have other articles that generate one to two leads per week, and even more articles that spin off leads every couple of weeks.

What I'm getting at here is this will be like a lead "annuity". Great content will send traffic and leads to your website traffic for years if you're producing valuable information that truly helps your customers.

Step #3: Acquire Inbound Links

An inbound link (also known as a backlink) is a hyperlink on a website that is directed towards your website. Inbound links help Google and other search engines determine how helpful and valuable your website is. Beyond valuable content, it's the most important ranking signal in the search engines.

Inbound links from trusted websites pointed to your website help your website to move up Google, Bing and Yahoo's search engine result pages (SERPs). To simplify it, think of it as a "vote of confidence" in your website. If you have a lot of "votes" from trusted websites, the search engines will believe you have valuable information and you'll see your rankings rise in the SERPs.

The first thing you should do is build your starter "brand" links. Start doing this only after you have your first 15 pages of content published.

The goal here is to build a few high-quality backlinks from big brand websites. These links send trust signals to Google and will help you withstand future algorithm updates.

This step includes building out your social profiles on Google, Facebook, YouTube and LinkedIn. It also includes building "Citations" to your website which are basically online directories. To see a suggested list of Starter Links, go to selltermlife.com/book-resources.

After you build those starter links, your website is ready for those sought-after, high-quality links (which are the missing piece of most life insurance agent websites). This is where you separate yourself from the rest of the agents in the search engines and get powerful rankings.

What you're going for here are "contextual editorial links". A contextual link is found in the main body of an article, where a set of related text is hyperlinked to a relevant site. The idea is that it's a natural link, surrounded by relevant content, that is designed to help readers of an article, NOT specifically to pass along link juice. Here's an example of a contextual editorial link from a Forbes.com article[3]:

> These mistakes can easily be avoided. Parents should create a life insurance trust for children that not only receives the money — no matter how old the child is — but **Contextual Link** ses. You can have the trust disburse specific amounts of the money at certain ages, like 25, 30 and 35.

Let's break this link down:

- The example article is linking to the URL "nerdwallet.com."

- The link to nerdwallet.com is coming from Forbes.com.

- The article containing the link is about finance and life insurance.

- The anchor text is "create a life insurance trust for children."

This is an awesome link for the nerdwallet.com site because...

- It comes from an authoritative domain.

- It is surrounded by relevant content.

- Has non-exact-match anchor text, but contains relevant words.

These are the type of links that are going to push you to the front pages of the search engines. It doesn't need to be Forbes—it can be a relevant blog, a local news website writing on a relevant topic etc. It just has to come from a domain with some authority

---

3 - http://www.forbes.com/sites/amydanise/2015/12/17/insiders-tips-buying-life-insurance/#30842d797e56

(more on this shortly).

Another thing you need to know about relevant contextual links... they're not easy to get.

If they were, they wouldn't be as valuable. Getting a high-authority, high-trust site in your niche (life insurance, scuba diving, burial insurance etc) to link to you naturally will bring you both natural, targeted traffic, and will increase the trust and authority of your own site—which directly helps you rank.

Because they are so valuable, everybody wants them. You can bet that authority sites that create these contextual links also know they're valuable, and don't give them away easily.

So now that you know what a contextual editorial link is, it's time to talk about getting some for your site.

As these links are not easy to get, it will take some time investment to go about getting one. Before you try any of these methods, you should make sure that your site looks good, and the content is relevant and high-quality. If a high-authority site links to your low-quality, no-value content, it's going to look bad on them. You'll have a much better chance of getting one of these links if you can convince someone at a glance that your site deserves to be linked to.

Here are some tried and true ways you can get contextual editorial links:

Help A Reporter Out (HARO)

This is my favorite shortcut and if you put in the effort, you'll start getting high authority contextual editorial links. I've been quoted in Forbes, Yahoo Finance and BusinessWeek along with many other high authority websites by using this service.

"Help A Reporter Out" is where a lot of media come to get quotes from experts. HARO connects you with these reporters.

You can visit Help A Reporter Out here: www.helpareporter.com

They send out several emails every day from reporters looking for expert sources on various topics. With their free version, you have to sift through a lot of different requests. I recommend subscribing to their "Advanced" version as you can filter for keywords like "insurance", "family" or "scuba divers" and more importantly you get the alerts before all the free subscribers get them.

Here's some more tips for using HARO:

- Respond quickly. The reporters are always on deadline and typically only source the first few that come in.

- Give the reporter everything they need so they don't need to reply back for more information and potentially miss their deadline. This includes your name, website and position.

- Respond to reporters' requests outside of life insurance—as getting a life insurance article request is pretty rare. For example, anything about entrepreneurship, using technology or anything where you can provide value. Think a little outside the box on this one.

- Be unique! Don't just give them the obvious answer to their query everyone else is giving them. They're getting a lot of responses, so make sure you stand out.

- Tell them who you are and why you're qualified to be their source.

Guest Post Outreach

Guest posting is simply writing an article for another website's blog. In doing so, you'll link back to your website.

Of course, you need to find those opportunities and that's where the real work and strategy comes in. And if you target the right websites, it could be a good source of qualified referral traffic as well.

Step 1: Make a Prospecting List of Websites to Target

First thing I would do is ask other agents you may know in the industry. I've guest posted on other life insurance agent's websites and vice-versa. Then look at other businesses you know and if they have a blog, see if you can write a relevant article.

After that exercise, Google the term: [keyword] "guest post" (for examples, Burial insurance "guest post", or Diabetics "guest post"). Putting guest post in quotation marks like this will ensure the search results only return sites with that exact phrase, so you don't have to sift through any irrelevant sites.

You'll get a list of websites that have accepted guest posts previously and those are your first targets. Go down the list and write the website name and contact information on a spreadsheet.

This is your new guest posting prospecting list.

Step 2: Pitch Your Guest Post

This is key. You have to know your guest posting target's audience if you want a good shot at getting published. Take a look at some previous guest posts that have been published.

What level is the audience are they writing for (beginner, advanced etc.)? What type of content do they publish? Is it mostly general concepts or specific tutorials?

From there, craft an email pitch that will go to the site's owner or content team. Here are some tips:

- Sometimes there will be guest posting guidelines— follow those guidelines.

- Personalize your email—look for the name of the person who will read your pitch, either on the website or social media accounts, and use it.

- A quick compliment on their website and what you like about it.

- Tell them the article you'd like to write for them and why. Let them know why their audience would get value from it.

- Link to some of your previous work.

That's it. Don't write your life's story, don't try to kill them with compliments. If they are truly a high-authority site, chances are they get lots of emails from people looking to appear on their site. If they don't respond, follow up at least four times. If you really want to get on their site, start commenting on their blogs or joining the conversation on social media as well.

Step 3: Deliver

If you do get the chance to guest post on a site, don't be obnoxious with how you link to your own site. Link naturally, in a way that enhances what you're writing about and adds to the reader experience, not in a gratuitous way that stands out. Link to other sites naturally as well. If your site is the only link, that's not quite natural.

Write a solid article—one that's long, in-depth, truly helpful, and link to your own site in a completely natural, relevant way. Give as much value as you can, and you have a good chance of getting the kind of link you're after.

A Cautionary Tale:

There are backlinking services all over the internet where you can pay someone to build backlinks for you. My warning is that the majority of these services will do more harm than good. Especially if they're affordable. No one can build you high authority, relevant backlinks unless you're paying a sizable amount.

You can outsource your backlinking, but you need to work with honest people and know what you're doing. I've seen some very bad things happen to agent's websites who partnered with the wrong company (including bans and penalties from the search engines). It's not worth the risk

Step #4: Optimize

Google will rank your site in the search results depending on your domain authority. Domain authority is determined by how many strong, relevant inbound links you have.

Irrelevant links, sparse or 'thin' content can detract from your domain authority. Google identifies these issues by tracking some simple metrics:

1. Click-through rates

2. Scroll rate (did users scroll below the fold?)

3. Time on page

4. Bounce rate

To ensure your domain authority is healthy, it's wise to perform some of the following 'SEO hygiene' on your site on a regular basis.

Optimize click-through rates

- Your page titles must 'sell the click'. Make your titles compelling and relevant to what people will be searching for.

- Your meta descriptions must also sell the click. Fill these out for each page, using interesting sales copy to get people to visit the page.

To make this process easier, we recommend installing a free WordPress plugin called Yoast. It gives you all the details for optimizing the titles and meta-data on each post.

Improve scroll rate

Write highly engaging, relevant content at the very beginning of each piece of content. Address the reason people are reading this post, so they know they're in the right place and will continue reading through to the end.

To do this, you can use an old writing formula:

1. Tell them what you're going to tell them.

2. Tell them.

3. Tell them what you told them.

It might sound simplistic, but it's powerful. Here's an example:

> *"In this article, you're going to learn about the best life insurance policies for scuba divers. You'll learn exactly what to ask for, what phrases to use with your broker, and which companies have the best policies....*
>
> *(Outline the information)*
>
> *You're now ready to go out and get a policy that is not negatively affected by your love of scuba diving. Using this information and working with these companies is the most effective way to get the coverage you need for total peace of mind."*

Increase average time on page

People invest their time before they invest their money. The longer you can keep them on each page, engaging them with your content, the more likely they'll be to use your services.

There are a few simple ways to do this. First, keep in mind that most people won't bother reading even the most interesting post if it's an unbroken block of text. Break up your content into bite-size paragraphs, bullet lists, and include pictures and break-out quotes as is appropriate. Use infographics—people spend more time absorbing them. Videos and sound recordings are also great for keeping people on the page longer.

Decrease bounce rate

Your bounce rate is the rate at which visitors land on your site, view one page and decide to go elsewhere.

We'll get into this in a bit more depth shortly, but speed is everything when it comes to engaging your readers. If your site is slow to load, they will click away faster than you can say life insurance policy. When people flee your site, your bounce rate will be extremely high. Google will assume your site is irrelevant or horrible for users, and drop your site down the rankings.

You can find out your page load speed at: https://developers.google.com/speed/pagespeed/insights. If your load speed is slow, consider moving your hosting, as this is often the culprit (unless you have a lot of videos or unoptimized images to load).

For our recommendations on hosting, visit selltermlife.com/book-resources. Hosting companies keep evolving and we'll keep the page updated with the most current, accurate information.

Digging Deeper: The Technical Framework of SEO

Sometimes when browsing the search engine rankings, you'll see certain sites rank highly even though their content and information is less thorough than yours.

This happens to life insurance agents constantly. They publish great content following all of the important rules, and yet they still don't get any real traffic or search visibility.

This happens because they don't understand the technical framework of SEO.

There are six core technical elements to ranking in the search engines. Once you understand these six elements, you'll understand how to get a website to rank in the search engines, beyond just writing great content:

1. The relevance of the page

2. Authority of the domain

3. Authority of inbound links

4. Relevance of inbound links

5. Mobile friendly

6. Website speed

Generally speaking, the webpage with the best combination of these core elements wins, so your goal is to increase the quality of every technical element. Right now, mediocre life insurance websites are ruling the search engines for life insurance terms. As long as you can be better than mediocre, you'll do great.

Technical Element #1: Page Relevance

Each piece of content you publish should have a specific purpose, based on your long-tail keywords. For example, if you're trying to rank for *"life insurance with arthritis"*, you want that information to be present in the title, description, content and links.

Here's what it might look like in the search results:

How to Get Affordable Life Insurance with Arthritis

Getting life insurance with arthritis can be tough, especially if you're trying to keep your premiums down. Click here to find out the best companies and policies for your situation.

Then when the reader clicks through to the post, you should include the phrase "life insurance with arthritis" somewhere in the first paragraph, and once or twice more throughout the rest of the content.

You should also include links to other relevant posts within your site and occasionally link out to other reputable sites.

It's very easy to modify your title, URL and post description within Wordpress (we use Yoast SEO to do this). The plugin will walk you through a tutorial, so you will be able to modify these areas easily and within seconds.

Most importantly—you need relevant content.

Your posts should be relevant, long-form content, ideally with 1000+ word counts.

Additionally, your internal link structure is *very* important and is often overlooked by life insurance agents' websites because it sounds intimidating. Simply put, it means you cluster the content on your site together strategically by interlinking your articles.

For example: your Indexed Universal Life Insurance articles should link together and they should link to your pillar Indexed Universal Life Insurance article.

Most of the life insurance content on the internet isn't optimized correctly because it's done by life insurance agents who don't know what they're doing. If you write long-form, relevant content, use the Yoast SEO plugin, and internally link your articles strategically, you'll see killer results.

Technical Element #2: Domain Authority

If you have a website and you're not getting any search engine traffic or leads, a lack of domain authority is most likely the reason. This is the hardest element to build, because it takes time and strategy.

The authority of your domain is created by links pointing at the domain. Specifically, the authority is built by a combination of the strength of those links, the total number of links and the diversity of your link profile.

It is also influenced by the length and number of pages on your website. This is why you see Forbes and LifeHappens.org (our industry's non-profit organization) topping out the rankings for various life insurance keywords.

Finally, authority is also built by social factors and the age of your content.

(You can check any domain's authority through Moz.com's Open Site Explorer. You don't need a subscription to Moz.com to check domain authority, but it will limit the amount of searches you can make per day.)

You need to build not only the authority of your domain, but also the authority of the page(s) you're trying to rank. This can be accomplished by building inbound links from other quality websites, which we'll discuss more below.

Relevant content is NOT enough to rank your pages. It has to be a combination of relevant content and domain authority.

Technical Element #3: Inbound Link Authority

This element refers to the power of the pages that the incoming links are on, the power of the domains the links are coming from, and the social signals the links have.

A link from a brand new website won't do much for your rankings unless, of course, that web site increases in authority. You want to get other strong websites linking to you, and you want the page within those websites linking to you to be strong as well.

Social signals are very important as well. There's power in having a link coming from a site that has active social media accounts associated with it.

You don't need to focus too much on this point at this stage, but remember that all links to your website are viewed differently. Just a few powerful links to your site can make a big difference.

Technical Element #4: Inbound Link Relevance

You want to have other *relevant* websites linking to your articles. A financial services site linking to your life insurance site is good. A spammy Viagra site linking to your life insurance site is bad.

If you're writing an arthritis article, getting a link from an arthritis site is great. So is a link from any financial services article or website.

A link from a mommy blogger who wrote an article about her struggle to secure life insurance is great, and so is a link from a CPA who wrote an article about life insurance.

Really, any website that writes a full article on arthritis or life insurance would be a great relevant link, especially if it's coming from a high-authority page.

You also have to factor in anchor text. Anchor text is the text in a hyperlink that can be clicked on. This is a ranking factor in the search engines for relevancy. In this example, you would want to rank for "no medical exam policy", so a link back to your website with this anchor text will tell Google it's highly relevant.

However, you don't want to over do it. If *all* of your links have your keyword in it, it looks unnatural and Google will most likely penalize you. Over-optimization is a rookie SEO mistake.

A good rule of thumb is to build a few anchor text links to your article for the keyword you're trying to rank. For everything else, just use whatever is natural—it could be your brand name, your website name, or call-to-action links.

Technical Element #5: Mobile Optimized Website

Mobile devices are your smartphones and tablets. Ensuring your site is mobile-friendly has become *very* important in search. Google needs your website to be mobile-friendly in order to maintain your rankings.

To put things into perspective, over 35% of my site's visitors come from mobile devices.

A lot of agents' websites are mobile friendly, but are *not* mobile optimized. Here's the difference: A life insurance website might pass Google's guidelines for being mobile friendly, but in reality many don't render correctly on a mobile device. The page load speed on mobile might be really slow and the quote forms might not show up correctly. This is off-putting to mobile users, and damages your conversion potential.

Technical Element #6: Website Speed

Back in 2010, Google announced pagespeed as a factor in ranking websites. The speed at which your website loads is actually a factor in ranking in the search engines.

The back-end performance of a website directly impacts search engine ranking. This includes web servers, network connections, the use of content display networks and the back-end application and database servers.

To most of us, this technical jargon is way over our heads. Fortunately, all you need to do is use a quality web host for your site, then run your website through https://developers.google.com/speed/pagespeed/insights and www.webpagetest.org when it's all set up.

If your website was built by a quality programming team and is on good hosting, your website should load quickly.

However, if those tools return any suggestions on how you can increase your page load speed, pay a developer to make the necessary changes. Don't try to do this yourself, as it's very technical and getting it wrong can negatively affect your website.

Finally, evaluate the results from webpagetest.org to see how fast your website loads. Your pages should take no longer than three seconds to load, although ideally it would be less than one second.

Not only is it important for your ranking in the search engines, but speed is everything when it comes to engaging your readers. If your site is slow to load, they will click away faster than you can say life insurance policy. As I mentioned earlier, when people flee your site, your bounce rate will be terrible, so Google will read that to mean that your site and content do not deserve to be listed high in the rankings.

If your load speed is slow, consider moving your hosting, as this is often the culprit (unless you have lots of videos or unoptimized images to load). WPEngine.com offers fast WP hosting, with up to 75% speed increase.

Creating the Perfect Storm

If you can build a relevant page, on a high domain authority website, with strong and relevant inbound links coming to that page, you'll eventually reach the top rankings in the search engines.

Those results are even easier to obtain if you have a mobile-optimized website.

If you take action to improve each of the six core elements we discussed on your chosen life insurance niche, you'll rank even better in the search engines.

The big life insurance companies with domain authority only target the big terms such as "term life insurance" and "life insurance quotes". They won't go after specific niches because of adverse selection. So that leaves almost every other search term open for independent life insurance agents.

Independent agents can target just about any niche and get results just by optimizing for the six core technical elements of SEO to their websites.

I can't stress enough how much success you can have, just by following the steps laid out here.

CHAPTER 9

Buying Traffic

Buying traffic to your website is a more advanced form of internet marketing. The content here will help you to understand the fundamentals, but instead of giving you all the strategies in-depth, I'll direct you to some great resources to learn more. Buying traffic is always changing and would date this book quickly.

One of the most common website woes I hear from agents is, *"I just don't have enough traffic to my site!"*

I have some good news: you actually don't have a traffic problem. Traffic is always available to buy if you want it.

What you have is one of the following:

1. Cash flow problem

2. Measurement problem

3. Process problem

4. Knowledge problem

5. Time commitment problem

In fact, you may have several of those problems.

Getting traffic is easy. Anyone can flash some money in the right place and turn on the traffic. Too many agents just don't understand the economics of *buying* traffic.

If you knew you could spend $1 and get $5 back, would you? Of course you would!

But most people don't know their numbers (a measurement problem). Most people don't have processes in place to consistently bring in those numbers (a process problem).

And most don't have the budget to test those numbers (a cash flow problem).

Others are intimidated by everything they don't know about advertising and marketing, or maybe they just don't want to spend the necessary time to really understand it. Those are the knowledge and time commitment problems.

The underlying problem of all these problems is an **unwillingness to take a risk**—to spend the cash, to put in the effort to learn marketing, or to invest time implementing the new knowledge.

There is so much information out there that will help you get you traffic if you seek it out and act on it. You just have to be willing to do it. Make sure you spend some time really digging into the foundational problem you're dealing with. *Then* you can tackle getting traffic to your website.

First, let's get really specific about what 'buying traffic' means. You can buy traffic several different ways: PPC, display advertising, Facebook advertising, and insurance ad networks.

You pay the platform you're advertising on to show your ads to prospects based on their searches, interests or browsing patterns. You can pay per impression, per click or per conversion.

Pay-Per-Click Advertising

Pay-Per-Click ("PPC") is a method of advertising, deployed on platforms like Google, Bing, Yahoo, Facebook and Twitter. You pay the platform a fixed amount per click, or even more specifically, per person who clicks on your ad as it shows up when they enter a particular search term.

These days, Google AdWords is the dominant PPC advertising platform. The enormous traffic volume from their site is able to deliver the most ad impressions and click-throughs of any system.

You can purchase front-page traffic for any search term out there—it just depends on how much you're willing to spend to get someone to your site.

Many people assume you must outspend your competition to get the best return on your ad spend, but it's not necessary. You can get great results with a relatively conservative ad spend.

There are many factors that determine the ads that appear on a page. You can create successful campaigns by optimizing the following:

- Keyword relevance
- Click-through rate

- Landing page quality
- Quality score (Google's combined rating of the quality and relevance of your keywords, landing pages, and PPC campaigns)

Again, Google doesn't just reward the highest bidders. They reward the ads with the *highest quality*. The more clicks your ad receives, the higher you will rank and the lower your costs will be. There's a lot more to it than just how much you spend.

Before you start to buy traffic, you'll need a high-converting landing page to send your traffic to.

A big mistake is sending paid traffic to your home page. You really need to send them to a specific landing page to help you capture their details, so you can add them to your marketing machine and convert them when they're ready.

Landing Pages

Your landing page should have:

1. A clear call to action to fill out a form or call. Don't include other competing links—remove your menu links and mute all the other distractions about you, your service etc. that may take away from them completing the form.

2. A short paragraph about why they should fill out your form. Keep it short and about what benefits them.

3. Show some carrier logos to help with trust building.

4. Use an image that's warm and evokes emotion. Images of families work really well.

Here's an example of a very high-converting landing page from Austin Insurance Group:

When buying traffic, start with the design shown above for your landing page and change the text to fit your business.

Now let's explore the platforms where you purchase the traffic that will go to these landing pages. If you implemented this strategy today, you could potentially have your first leads coming in tomorrow.

Google Adwords

We'll start with Google AdWords, since it has the most traffic available for you to buy. It's also some of the most expensive traffic, if you don't know what you're doing. I recommend taking an in-depth Google Adwords course before sending any traffic to your website. Or alternatively, you can hire someone to set up your Adwords campaigns for you.

I know of several agencies placing over one million dollars of premium every year using Google AdWords as their sole source of traffic. Each of them are targeting a specific demographic or niche that they're very competitive in. Each of them will tell you that it takes a lot of effort to optimize the keywords you're targeting, ad copy, message and landing page, but if you crack the code, you'll have a lead machine.

To start running PPC campaigns on Google, head over to Google Adwords. Here's what the home page will look like:

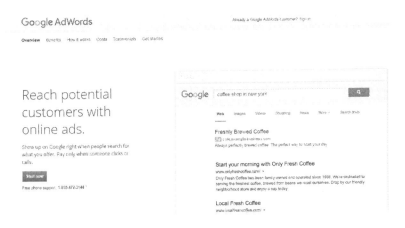

Click the 'Start Now' button on the left. Add your business website and email address, and then you'll be directed to a page where you can start setting up your first campaign (which is simply an ad or set of ads built around a particular theme, like life insurance for scuba divers).

Here are the steps for setting up a campaign:

1. **Set your daily budget.** If you set a budget of $10 per day, and your ad gets $10 worth of clicks by 12pm, the ad will simply stop showing until the next day, when the budget resets.

2. **Set your geographic locations.** You'll want to select the United States only, and niche down even further to show only to the states in which you are licensed.

3. **Choose your network.** For your first campaign, your ad will automatically show in the search engine results, but you can also choose to have it show on Google's affiliated sites if you wish.

4. **Add your keywords.** These are the specific search terms you want to trigger your ad. For example, you want to show up for "life insurance for scuba divers", not "health insurance" or something unrelated to your offer. Be as specific as possible with your terms so you only get people who are interested in exactly what you're offering.

5. **Set your maximum cost-per-click.** This is the maximum amount you're willing to spend to get a single person to click your ad. Once you've been running ads for a while, you'll be able to make better use of this (since you'll know what your conversion rates are, and therefore how much you can spend to acquire a customer), but for the time being it's best to accept the number Google suggests here.

6. **Write your ad. There are a few key elements:**

   » A snappy, attention-grabbing headline (don't try to be clever or funny—keep it simple and short. You get 25 characters.), e.g.—*Are You Scuba Insured?*

   » Include the keyword selected earlier. You get two lines of ad copy, with 35 characters per line: *Trouble getting life insurance / because of scuba? Click here.*

   » Has a clear call to action and directs the lead to a landing page.

Once you've set up your campaign, you'll be taken to the billing page to make it official.

After confirming your details and processing your payment, you can either set the campaign live, or pause it while you look around the rest of the Adwords platform. This is really up to you, but I recommend going through the guided tour Google will offer you, and then taking a formal training course or hiring a Google Adwords specialist to manage your campaign.

Now you're set up and understand the goals of the AdWords ecosystem, you can start running ads targeting different keywords. Make sure you further familiarize yourself with Google's guidelines so you can run as many campaigns as you want over time.

Maintenance

If you want to hit a homerun with your PPC campaign, you have to continuously optimize *everything*. Test your headlines. Review your keyword relevance. Refine your landing page.

Before you start your own campaign, use an intelligence tool like SEMrush or WhatRunsWhere to find out what ads your competition have been running. If they've been running the same ads for over a year, you know that the copy and keywords are working for them.

Start by checking out the big guys, especially when it comes to landing page optimization. You'd be surprised how many of the big spenders in life insurance have landing pages that just aren't any good. With persuasive content and a clear call to action, yours can easily be better.

When done and maintained properly, PPC can be one of the most valuable tools used to grow your lead base and increase your ROI. And don't forget—you want to focus on a core demographic or niche where you're strong.

If you specialize in helping federal employees, bid on those terms only. If it's scuba divers, bid on those terms that will go directly to your scuba diver's life insurance landing page. Make sure you have a high chance of converting the leads that come in by focusing on areas where you have a competitive edge.

Display Advertising

Display advertising comes in several forms, but the most common variation you will see is the banner ad on a high-traffic site. These ads generally rely on images, audio, and video to attract their market.

While PPC is great for targeting people who are currently researching life insurance, this kind of advertising puts you in front of people who *aren't* yet in the buying process, but *are* in your market segment. With display advertising, you choose to target the demographics of these people, and doing so will create plenty of steady, targeted traffic to your site.

Like PPC, you have to maintain consistency with display advertising. You'll get the most value from the people who continually see your ads on the sites they visit and eventually decide it's time to make a move.

If you're going to try display advertising, I recommend sticking with it for at least six months. It takes a while to get your messaging and creative (visuals to go with your ads) perfected, but once you've got it dialed in, you could be sitting on a gold mine. I know a number of agents who have gotten such a steady flow of high-converting leads that they've been running the same ads for more than three years in the same places.

To bring this concept into reality, here's a couple of examples from agencies using display advertising effectively. I changed the actual niche and sources to protect their identities.

Display Advertising Example #1

There's a niche-specific life insurance agency with two agents targeting scuba divers. They've been advertising on the biggest scuba diving daily newsletter for over three years now and haven't missed a single day.

This niche agency is spending over $300 per day to get that banner ad placement (display advertising). They're competing with several other display advertisements on that email, though none of them are offering life insurance. They're spending over $110,000 per year just to advertise to this specific niche, and if they haven't missed a day in three years, it must be working really well.

This life insurance agency is leveraging the email newsletter of a trusted company in their niche to build their business through display advertising. It didn't start working right away, but over time they were able to build trust with the audience thanks to their consistency. They also made sure they optimized their messaging and ad copy, and soon enough had built a profitable referral source.

Think about how many niches out there you could apply this to. Once you have a list of opportunities, find out if they have trusted associations, non-profits or educational websites you can advertise on, and start building relationships with those potential partners.

Display Advertising Example #2

This one is really simple. There's an agency that purchases display advertising in the finance section of a conservative website, as well as coverage in the email newsletter that goes out to the site's subscribers.

This is the main lead source for this four-agent call center. The financial news site sends them over 1,500 high-quality leads every month.

The cost of advertising on this website is high, and most agencies would balk at the price. However, the readership is affluent, likely to buy, and willing to spend a lot on the right coverage. In the end, the revenue generated from each client more than justifies the high cost per lead.

Facebook Advertising

Many agents are skeptical about buying ads on a social media site, but Facebook is a legitimate and high-converting traffic source if used well. It's the cheapest source of traffic you can buy right now, *and* your prospects are already spending their time there.

Facebook ads can be laser-targeted to certain demographics. You could drill down so far that you only target your ad toward women in a particular city, over a certain age, who own a home, and who like peanut butter and jelly sandwiches. I'm not kidding about how specific Facebook can be.

To put this into perspective, there's an agent I know who generates, on average, five new annuity appointments every single week directly from Facebook. **Not leads—actual appointments.**

He has a sophisticated sales funnel. He drives Facebook traffic to a landing page to download a free guide, and then follows up with a very compelling email series that convinces and qualifies the prospects who downloaded the guide to set an appointment.

There's another agency I know that targets burial insurance strictly from Facebook Ads. They target the 50+ age demographic within a geographical area, and send them to a burial insurance landing page. They spent a few months optimizing the Facebook targeting, ad copy, images and landing page, and now they can turn leads on and off as they wish.

Like any advertising, you need to learn how to work the platform. Facebook ads demand strong images, a great call-to-action, clear copy, and an attractive landing page. Visit selltermlife.com/ book-resources for our recommended Facebook Ads training courses.

Insurance Ad Networks

Though few agents know these exist, insurance ad networks have been becoming more popular. These are typically high-traffic websites that sell clicks through an ad network.

A lead vendor, for example, may offer a lead three to five suggestions of other places they can go to get quotes after filling out an online form. The lead vendor sells these clicks to external landing pages.

To best explain how it works, let me show you how insurance ad networks are sending traffic to agents' websites.

A life insurance prospect will go to a website and read an article about life insurance, then they'll see this:

When you type in your zip code, a bunch of options will show up like this:

You can bid for those listings above. You can determine the time of day you want to place your bids, the zip code range and the text to display on these ads to get the most relevant and qualified traffic.

Any time you see a life insurance article that asks for a zip code only, you can advertise on that website through an insurance ad network.

Depending on the website and competition, you'll be paying anywhere from $2 to $10 per click, which translates to agents generating leads for $10 to $30 per lead. It just depends on your settings within the ad network and your conversion percentages.

Some best practices for insurance ad networks:

- Get familiar with the settings on the insurance ad network and set them up so you're only getting traffic in the states in which you're licensed.

- Monitor your results every day. Remove your advertising from websites that aren't converting well.

- Test your ad copy on the listing page and on the landing page to which you're sending the traffic.

- Send your traffic to a high-converting landing page, as mentioned previously.

It's not as simple as just getting the ad live and sending traffic to your website. Don't use insurance ad networks unless you're willing to spend some money to bring your cost per lead down to an acceptable or profitable level.

Here are some basic insights as you dive into these insurance ad networks:

- Look at what other agencies are using for copy on their ad and start from there, but get specific on what you offer.

- You'll see you'll pay less for leads generated after hours because there's less competition. The broader area you can cover, the more opportunities for clicks and traffic you'll get.

Insurance ad networks have come and gone over the years. Head over to selltermlife.com/book-resources and we'll list the current insurance ad networks you can advertise on.

Too many agents assume that PPC doesn't work and is too expensive because they're not optimizing. They're not putting the time into researching relevant keywords and they're linking ads to their homepage. The great thing about buying traffic is that it's a consistent flow, so it really helps you get to know your numbers. And of course, with further optimization, you can make it more and more profitable over time.

Affiliate and Affinity Marketing

Nic West, an agent who mentored me on this skill set, has shared everything in this section to teach you how to get started building affiliate and affinity marketing opportunities. His insights here can have a profound impact on your business.

There are many ways to partner with marketers and established websites to provide them with life insurance offers. This goes far beyond just paying these websites for advertising or on a pay-per-lead basis.

As a lead buyer, Nic aims to spend less than 30% of the premiums he makes on customer acquisition. When you look at the commission cycle of life insurance, it takes several months to get your money back, let alone to turn a profit from the investment. Diversifying with free lead sources allows your business to function without having to spend a lot of money on acquiring customers.

Affinity Partners

An affinity group is a collection of agents who sell different products to similar clients. For example, if you sell life insurance and don't offer health insurance, you can team up with a health insurance agent who doesn't offer life insurance. You can share leads, split the revenue, and do right by the client by offering them more lines of insurance with very little extra effort.

Forming affinity partnerships like this can be a lifeline for a growing business. Life insurance agents who operate online are focused on finding the next sale, marketing themselves, buying leads, and building traffic. Nic believes that you have much better things to do with your time than dealing with lead sellers and bogus lead returns.

When he got started, Nic spent a couple of hours each day calling health insurance agencies, property and casualty firms, and other complementary associations to establish a revenue-sharing agreement for shared leads. He still does this in his business today. These agencies have the clients he wants, he has the skills they want, and together they can service clients for a variety of insurance products.

Good affinity partners include health agencies, P&C agencies, financial advisors, and Medicare agents. Typically, you'll find that life insurance agencies don't want to learn new products lines, so it's easier to stick with parallel products. And while many of these affinity partners do offer life insurance, their knowledge is limited. In these cases, it pays to be their go-to agent for the more complex or difficult cases they need help with.

PBLA: "Performance-Based Lead Agreement"

On a call one day, Nic came up with the Performance-Based Lead Agreement ("PBLA"). In short, he would cut a deal to pay for leads based on performance (determined by contact rate, bogus rate, and ultimately premium and revenue). The lead generator would get paid depending on the quality of the leads they sent, which ensured they had some skin in the game and therefore would have no incentive to generate or send bogus leads. The lead generator would not get paid if there was no performance.

In some cases, Nic would pay 30% on PBLAs as a lead stipend, tied to revenue. Since it is a gray area to only pay for leads that result in a sale, he would pay 30% of his revenue, divided by the block of leads it took to get there. A lead could cost $15 or $50, depending on the performance of the source.

One way to set up your own PBLAs is to find websites that display life insurance offers that lead to an obvious "lead gen" page. This kind of set-up shows that the original website is getting paid per lead, or per click. You can approach that website, find out what deal they're currently on, and then put together a more lucrative PBLA offer. They will then want to promote your service instead, because they stand to earn more, and know their visitors will be taken care of.

Another real-world example of a PBLA in action is an agency that partnered with a diabetic supply company.

At the end of each call, the diabetic supply company would ask the client:

"Are you interested in speaking with our partner who specializes in helping diabetics secure the lowest possible premiums for life insurance?"

If the answer was yes, the client's information would be transferred over to the life insurance agency's CRM for follow-up and tracking. This particular example resulted in over 1,200 leads per month for the agency that paid the diabetic supply company according to their PBLA.

Finding a good PBLA can explode your business. Spending your time prospecting for these types of agreements can be very profitable, and while they do take some time to develop, there's no reason an agent or agency could not build their entire business with PBLAs.

Associations

Associations are a gold mine for leads. It takes time to establish relationships with them, but they will become valuable, long-term relationships if you can provide real value to their members.

Associations are heavily focused on retention. They retain their members by providing them access—as a group—to discounts, programs, and insurance offers that offer some form of perceived exclusivity.

Think about some of the associations that exist, like NAIFA, the NRA or AARP. These associations market relentlessly to sell products, or have their members donate money, sign up for an email list, click on a link, etc. They make money on a lot of what their members buy through their funnel, *and there is no difference in the insurance transactions being offered through associations.*

Facilitating a partnership with an association is actually quite easy if you can clearly demonstrate your value. Setting up an actual campaign is a little more difficult, since you have to work through the compliance aspects, but the association will give you guidelines on exactly what you can and can't do.

The typical process is to run the campaign online, set up a co-branded landing page and send any business through to a fulfillment center (sometimes a one-man operation, or a multi-agent call center).

If you are introduced to an association, ask about their retention, what products they are offering, what kind of revenue sharing agreements they have with their current marketing partners, and if they have an appetite for making $300 to 500 revenue per sale product. You'd be surprised how many associations and memberships organizations are insurance licensed for this reason.

Typical Splits

As long as everyone is getting paid appropriately for their role in the relationship, there is no right or wrong answer as to what the splits should be.

A typical split is a third to the lead source, a third to sales person, and a third to the processing and marketing support firm that provides all the infrastructure. If the split is between an agent and an association, the split is typically 50/50 of the agents' commission level.

If the entity is not licensed, it turns into a lead purchasing or "PBLA" closer to the 20-30% range, paid as a marketing stipend to the association. Some associations prefer commissions if they are licensed, while some are not licensed and prefer selling leads. Check your state law before entering into a revenue sharing agreement.

Case Study

In 2012, I began a relationship with a P&C agency that wrote very little life insurance. I worked closely to establish trust with them by calling on their low-level clients. Gradually I worked my way up to their "A-level" clients, and was referred a buy-sell lead.

I called and closed the deal in 30 minutes, to 19 employees of a stock redemption buy-sell arrangement. It was $144,000 of premium, and I walked away with $42,000 in commissions. The P&C agent was floored. He had been sitting on this account and had no idea the commission potential. Needless to say, he has referred plenty more business.

In short, diversification is key to long term survival in this business.

Diversifying lead sources is one of the best business decisions you could ever make. As long as each relationship you establish is fair and mutually beneficial, it is hard not to make money over the long term. One good relationship can explode your business. If you make it about the clients, the commissions will follow.

CHAPTER 10

Ongoing Growth Strategies

At this point, you have the tools and resources to grow a profitable internet based life insurance business. You're familiar with the aspects of creating a website and marketing strategy that will bring leads into your business and you have the scripts and tools to convert those into customers. Now let's dig into some business growth strategies to make sure all this momentum continues into the future.

Do The Work That Matters

Moving your business is a choice that demands action—constant, determined, all-in action. If your commitment dwindles, your previous efforts are wasted. **Mindset is everything.**

To have real, increasing success as an online life insurance agent, you must commit to the following:

- One to two hours of study and implementation **daily**

- Did I mention learning and implementing **every day**?

- Do at least this much for **12 months** and keep it up even after this initial period.

I have never met an agent who has a successful online life insurance business who hasn't made this kind of study a daily habit.

Take action every day for a year. You won't succeed otherwise.

Key Performance Indicators

Make no mistake. You're in a sales and marketing business. You may be the best insurance advisor in the nation, but if you can't learn to market or sell with the new technology available, then you won't be able to help many people.

When running a business of any kind, you must always keep a pulse on the sales and marketing. These two elements provide the most critical insights and opportunities for growing your business.

Key performance indicators (KPIs) are used by all sorts of companies to track progress toward various goals. As long as your KPIs keep getting better and business is growing, then commissions will follow.

Focusing on improving KPIs one at a time will make you a better business owner and a more profitable life agent.

In life insurance, there are so many variables which can affect your income. At the very least you should be tracking the most important ones. It's not just about placed annual premium and lead costs. There are dozens of ways to make your business more profitable.

Here's a list of basic KPIs every life insurance agent should be tracking every month:

Basic Sales KPIs

- Total annual premium of applications taken.

- Total number of applications taken.

- Total annual premium placed (applications placed in force).

- Total number of applications placed.

- Average premium per sale.

You should constantly strive to increase all five of these numbers. Categorize these KPIs by lead source and analyze them month over month. This will show you trends in your business that indicate how healthy your pipeline is, and if there is any part of the funnel which is causing bottlenecks.

Make sure you're also keeping an eye on the ratios, particularly your number of applications taken to number of applications placed. You should be placing at least 50% of the applications you take. Even if you're above that number, work on getting it better. The higher your ratio, the more money you make!

To increase your own placement ratio, you can work on qualifying your leads a little better, building more trust, or tying them down to the sale. There could be a number of issues causing a poor placement ratio, but you won't know it's a problem unless you're tracking your sales KPIs.

Basic Marketing KPIs

- Total lead count.

- Bogus lead count (and good:bad ratio).

- Total marketing costs (lead costs + money spent on marketing) .

Again, categorize these by the lead source for accurate reporting.

You should be monitoring your lead count and marketing costs like a hawk. Know how much you're spending per lead source and cross reference these numbers to your sales KPIs.

(We do this by combining the data in tracker reports, which we discuss later in this chapter.)

Part of this is also tracking the quality of the leads, by dissecting your leads and categorizing them into good and bogus. A bogus lead is one that contains completely useless information, leaving no way to contact the person. However, if a lead has a bad phone number but a good email address, this isn't a bogus lead, only low quality.

By knowing these marketing and sales KPIs, you can track your acquisition costs and calculate how much it costs to acquire a new client.

The cost of acquiring an in-force policy is a very valuable piece of information if used in correlation with your average in-force premium. Would you pay $250 to place $1000 in-force? I would! I would do it all day, every day, and double down as much as my cash flow allowed. But you have to know your numbers and make sure they're consistent before you can scale.

Sales Activity KPIs

- Total calls made.

- Total contacts (conversations).

- Total prospects qualified and quoted.

You can track this easily if you're using a sales CRM. If you're using a basic CRM which doesn't track this, you can track it manually, but I wouldn't worry too much about it.

Marketing Activity KPIs

- Amount of 1,000+ word articles written (if doing content marketing).

- Amount of quality links acquired (if doing content marketing).

- Total PPC costs per click and per lead.

- Conversion rates.

I mentioned earlier in the book that content marketing and SEO are a great foundation to any independent life insurance agent's business. If you can make sure you're hitting these KPIs every month, your lead flow and income will grow over time.

At a very minimum, track the marketing KPIs above. There are a lot of other key performance indicators, like traffic growth or conversion percentages, but these are the foundational numbers.

Keep the above numbers in a spreadsheet and look at trends every month. See where you're falling short or where you're accelerating. Get a pulse on where you can improve or become more consistent.

Run your business and make decisions about your business based on this data.

On top of KPIs, there are also reports you can run from within your CRM which can help you visualize your own recent activity and its direct correlation to your success.

We run two types of reports in our agency to track these KPIs: a *tracker report* and an *activity report*.

A tracker report tracks what has happened with each individual lead. In other words, the data of where a lead or group of leads currently stands.

An activity report is what happened within a certain timeframe based on an agent's actions.

Tracker Reports

Here's an example of our tracker report. On January 20th I ran a tracker report for Jan 1—Jan 15 for a data set of 204 leads:

- Leads received: 204
- Total Calls: 760
- Sales Made: 10
- Sale Rate of Leads: 4.9%
- Call Ratio: 3.72
- Premium Placed: $3250

If I ran this same report on March 1st, five weeks after running the last report, to let that same data (from Jan 1—Jan 15) cycle through the sales process of attempting contact and follow ups, the same set of leads may now look like this:

- Leads received: 204
- Total Calls: 1629
- Sales Made: 15
- Sale Rate of Leads: 7.3%
- Call ratio: 7.98
- Premium placed: $6200

The numbers improved because there was more time to sell and let our contact attempts and follow-ups cycle through.

On April 1st, a full month later, if I ran the same data (Jan 1-Jan 15), the numbers would get bigger again.

You can only get your true bottom-line numbers after a significant time frame, and if you have enough data to work with. Once you have those numbers, you can determine what happens with each lead source and make decisions based on those metrics.

At times it might appear as though a particular lead source isn't producing enough placed premium. Looking at a tracking report, though, might reveal that the leads were only called a few times, or that the lead source hasn't had enough time to cycle through all the calls.

This example illustrates that it's a problem in the sales process, not in the lead source.

A massive mistake agents make is only giving a lead source a couple of weeks to determine its profitability. Make sure you give every lead source at least 90 days after the last lead received to cycle through the attempting contacts and follow-ups before making a decision about profitability.

Activity Reports

An activity report tracks what happened within a certain time frame. You can see if you're having activity problems (not enough calls), lead quality issues (not a lot of contacts per lead), or lead flow problems or influxes (too little or too many leads coming in). Maybe you're just not making enough calls.

Here's what an activity report might look like for one week:

- Leads: 140
- Calls made: 625
- Contacts: 60

- Quoted: 22

- App out: 6

- App out premium: $6800

An agent can evaluate their selling activity by reviewing the activity report. If they didn't sell much last week, they can determine if there weren't enough calls made, if there was trouble getting in contact with people, or if the agent was quoting a lot of prospects but not closing the sale.

If you're an independent agent, look at these trends at least month over month. If you're running a small agency, look at these trends week over week.

Here are more advanced KPI's to track:

- Exam completion percentage.

- Percentage of AOTA.

- AOTA to Paid Percentage.

- Average cycle time per carrier.

- Placement ratio by lead source.

- Average premium placed by lead source.

Cash Flow

Managing your cash flow can make or break your business.

It doesn't matter if your commissions are at $1,000 a month, or $50,000 a month, you need to manage where you spend your marketing dollars closely.

For me, it comes down to where I will get the best *returns on cash flow*, and what risks I am willing to take, based on expected volatility and likelihood of success. I say 'returns on cash flow' instead of 'ROI', 'commissions' or 'revenue', because cash flow is what keeps a business growing TODAY.

In other words, I'd rather make a $1000 non-med sale with an advance that's paid next week, than a $1200 FUW placed policy paid as earned. This is because the cash flow I have to re-invest will generate more income to me by the time the as-earned policy finishes paying out.

I allocate more of my marketing dollars every month to the best cash flow investment first.

The business's cash position should be the primary factor in how much you invest in new projects or leads.

Here's an example I see constantly: Many agents have multiple websites. Some have half-completed websites because their cash flow didn't allow for their completion, or they don't have the cash flow to market it. Their website just sits there, when the time and money they spent could have gone into something that would actually generate revenue for their business. I always recommend that they find a way to finish their website and start making their money back.

Knowing your cash flow situation will make you a more efficient marketer. You'll make better decisions, focus on higher-yield opportunities, and see greater returns on your campaigns.

Now, being a life insurance agent, we're hit hard by not getting paid for approximately 60 days after submitting an application. This can kill cash flow, so we need to work smarter to overcome it.

Here are some tips to help you manage your cash flow so you're never short, and able to keep acquiring new leads through all your marketing channels.

Accounting Software

Use accounting software and track every lead purchase, marketing expense, state license purchase, commissions, and any other money that flows in and out of your business. Reconcile your accounts every month so you have a clear picture of your finances.

I use QuickBooks, but there are many other accounting tools that work just fine.

Accounting generates ROI. I know it sounds a bit crazy. It's just crunching numbers, right? Wrong.

If you show me a business that hasn't done it's books in two years, I'll show you a business that's underperforming. Without proper accounting you can't manage your cash flow effectively, which limits your ability to source good leads, create profitable advertising campaigns and act on opportunities that may come your way.

Advances

Instead of prospecting face-to-face, we're marketing online. Even though there are some free channels that can get you started, you need money to really get traction. At the very least, you will want to buy ads at some point. The more money you have, the more ads you can buy, and the more customers you can get.

While it's nice to have money coming in every month from your as-earned payments, getting advances gives you cash flow *now*. Even if you're not ready to buy ads right away, you can use that cash to reinvest in your business, earning more revenue in the time it would take to collect the earnings from your as-earned sales.

Don't worry about chargebacks. If you're selling correctly, they're rare. Plus, you're doing a high volume of sales anyway, so it's not a big problem.

Non-Med Policies

Non-med policies get issued faster than other products, and you get paid quicker. This is key in helping with cash flow. Learn the top products, know their application systems and always bring it up as an option if it makes sense for the client.

(For a list of the top non-med life insurance products internet agents are writing, visit selltermlife.com/book-resources)

Business Credit Cards

Use a business credit card and pay it off every month. *You're buying yourself 30 extra days of cash flow.* Since it takes, on average, 60 days to get paid on a fully underwritten policy from the time it's sold, you'll improve your cash flow by delaying the marketing dollars coming out of your account by 30 days.

Not only that, but you'll accumulate points for travel! I booked round-trip first-class tickets to Europe for my family, just by using a rewards credit card for my business expenses. If this is a new idea to you, check out this post (once you've done your marketing for the day, obviously):

- http://chrisguillebeau.com/travel-hacking-resources

Lead Reports

Use your CRM or keep an Excel spreadsheet of your lead sources. For each lead source, keep track of how many applications are submitted, how much annual premium is submitted, how many are bogus, how many follow ups you have to make, etc.

You can then compare those numbers to other lead sources, and use this information to determine where you should be allocating the bulk of your marketing budget. You will see right away if a particular source is outperforming the others, or if it is a total waste of time.

It will take you a few months to get enough data for it to make a pattern, so don't throw away a channel if it doesn't crush it the first month. As you get better at marketing, the patterns you see here will become more and more reliable, and eventually you'll know exactly what works for your niche and what doesn't.

Block of Business Management

There's a lot of emphasis on drumming up new business in our industry, but the key to longevity is managing your block of business. According to InforcePro (which sees a lot of data from the life insurance companies):

Life insurance owners buy life insurance seven times over their lifetime, from six different agents.

There are two important statistics here.

The first is that over a lifetime, a person who owns life insurance will buy an average of seven times! This can be due to rewrites, lapses, adding or decreasing coverage, conversions, buying other life products or any number of situations.

The second important statistic is that they're buying from different agents the majority of the time, which means we're not doing a very good job of managing our blocks of business. We've all been told to do annual policy reviews, but not many agents actually do it.

I've found the most effective strategy here is to get in front of your clients during important policy events and life events.

Some key times to contact your client include:

- When their conversion option is coming up or when their conversion to the best permanent product available is coming up.

- Beneficiary change. What happened? New child? Divorce?

- Zip code change. Did they buy a new house? Did they move into a wealthier zip code?

Now, how are you supposed to know these events? We use InforcePro. Their dashboard serves up each of these events for dozens of carriers.

By contacting our clients during these changes, we increase our Customer Lifetime Value.

Customer Lifetime Value ("CLTV" or "CLV") is the amount of money each customer will spend with you over the entire duration of your professional relationship. If you sell each customer a single policy, your CLTV will be drastically lower than if you sell each customer all seven of those policies they're likely to buy.

Knowing, and then increasing, your CLTV is critical to the health of any business, but particularly when you're operating online.

If you know how much you can expect to earn from each customer, you also know how much you can spend to acquire them. Increasing CLTV will generate significantly more revenue and create real longevity in your business.

Hustle and Keep Learning

Hustling is about being resourceful and accomplishing a lot without much cash or influence to help you get started.

Marketing online is an uncharted area for most life insurance agents. You're going to be very humbled in the beginning, but you have to take every new lesson in stride and keep coming back focused and determined every day.

Even as you learn and start generating consistent business online, you're going to come across bigger challenges. That's the nature of a growing business—you overcome one obstacle, only to find yourself faced with a bigger one.

Ask for Help

If you can't find the answer to something yourself, don't be afraid to seek help. When you get into your office every day, ask yourself:

"What don't I know? Who can teach it to me?"

Then pursue the knowledge until it's yours. Cultivate mentors, connect with other people seeking similar knowledge, and keep up to date with how the online marketing sphere evolves.

This sounds obvious, but most life insurance agents shy away from this part of the process because of their egos or insecurities.

It's difficult. It's humbling to realize that you don't always have the answers.

But muddling through and just 'trying to make it work' is counterproductive. Face up to what you need to learn, then commit to doing it every day. Before long, you'll know exactly what you need to do, and how to do it. At that point, you're going to see significant results that can change the direction of your business.

This is how I continue to grow my internet life insurance business. I'm learning every single day, maintaining relationships with other smart agents who can teach and inspire me, and staying focused on growing a business that gives me the income, freedom and time to live how I want.

CONCLUSION

Time to Get Started

As I've watched agents make this transition in their businesses and in their lives, I've seen successful implementation of two models in particular:

1. The hybrid business

2. The 100% online business

The Hybrid Business

Many agents like to ease into a fully online business by first establishing somewhat of a hybrid business. They may continue to earn their living using conventional prospecting strategies, face-to-face sales, and seeking personal referrals. But with the intent to eventually weed out these practices, they will start moving towards applying the marketing strategies and building their website.

This may sound more comfortable for you than moving everything online, at least at first. But even if you're not moving your business entirely online, it is critical that you put in the time to fully educate yourself about the process.

Taking *any* amount of your life insurance business online is a commitment to the long game.

You can't expect to put a website up, write a few articles, and instantly see big results. It takes time, patience, and a consistent effort to get the momentum of an online business going.

You *don't* have to give up what you're currently doing in order to learn what fits well into your business, dig in deeper, and start implementing the strategies discussed in this book.

The 100% Online Business

This is the business I run. I generate my leads online and contact them over the phone.

There's no denying that prospecting is the most uncomfortable requirement of our job. But if you can decisively commit the time to learn every day, **you'll never have to prospect again.**

Running your business online reverses the paradigm—your marketing becomes inbound rather than outbound. Your leads seek *you*, pre-warmed. They submit a form to you when they're ready to get down to brass tacks, so you end up communicating on *their* terms.

An Important Note

These days, you can expect to encounter a lot of pushback about direct-to-consumer online marketing. Trainers of traditional life insurance marketing have long resisted catering to the changes happening in the industry. Resisting change is human nature.

The industry, however, is experiencing change as more and more people are going online to research their options and seek quotes. We as independent agents would be foolish not to change the way we operate in order to take advantage of it.

Throughout all of this, it's important to remember that you don't need to be number one. You don't need to be the first agent appearing on a Google search for quotes. You don't need to be paying the most for clicks.

You just need to be visible for when people are ready to take action.

That's why speed matters.

Choosing a business name, writing a perfect article, knowing the details of certain products... None of it matters as much as consistently taking action.

When it comes to mastering new skills, we all start from zero. It's the ability to stick with it that will set you apart from the crowd and propel you toward long-term, ongoing success.

Make decisions, execute, look forward, move forward, don't second guess, and just keep going.

You can be one of the agents building some serious wealth just by positioning yourself correctly in front of your target markets. Get your business seen by the niche audiences you're strongest with, the ones you can cater to with your products. That is where implementing online marketing strategies will take you far.

• • •

If you want to learn more and join a community of agents building big books of life insurance from the comfort of their homes and offices, join our email list over at SellTermLife.com.